SUPERNATURAL SIGNS, SYMBOLS, AND CODES

SUPERNATURAL SIGNS, SYMBOLS, AND CODES

Arlene Billings and Beryl Dhanjal

ROSEN
PUBLISHING®

New York

This edition first published in 2012 by:

The Rosen Publishing Group, Inc.
29 East 21st Street
New York, NY 10010

Additional end matter copyright © 2012 by
The Rosen Publishing Group, Inc.

Library of Congress Cataloging-in-Publication Data

Dhanjal, Beryl.
Supernatural signs, symbols, and codes/Beryl
Dhanjal, Arlene Billings.
    p. cm.—(The supernatural)
Includes bibliographical references
(p.   ) and index.
ISBN 978-1-4488-5987-0 (library binding)
1. Symbolism. 2. Supernatural.
I. Billings, Arlene. II. Title.
BF1623.S9B55 2012
130—dc23
                              2011031823

Manufactured in the United States of America

CPSIA Compliance Information: Batch #W12YA: For further
information, contact Rosen Publishing, New York, New York, at 1-
800-237-9932.

Arlene Billings, editor

CONTENTS

INTRODUCTION TO SYMBOLISM

We take the most important symbols for granted: our alphabets. For most of history, few people have been able to read. Gregory the Great (Pope, 590–604) urged iconographic and allegorical painting so *"those who know no letters may yet read."*

Renaissance philosophers did not value writing. They created symbols, charts, tables, and diagrams that were attempts to pin down all knowledge. Some occultists thought that a symbol acquired power of its own, the more so if the symbol was secret and the greatest if it was never discovered. (But then how would one know?)

Scientific thought was to challenge this. It was time for demystification. Translation of the Rosetta Stone undoubtedly helped the view that the creation of an alphabet was a complex human achievement and real magic. As J. R. R. Tolkien said, "Small wonder that spell means both a story told, and a formula of power over living men." Scholars took to prose, experiments, and textual studies.

As late as the mid-18th century, the alphabet was seen as destructive to morals and language. At this time, about half of the British could read, a great achievement of Protestantism and humanism, but the spread of literacy was viewed as potentially disastrous. One source of alarm was the appearance of the first novels with heroes and heroines of questionable

ABOVE: Pope Gregory the Great wanted his message to be clear to all, through art.

OPPOSITE ABOVE LEFT: What does the rose mean to you?

OPPOSITE ABOVE RIGHT: Augusta, Sicily—a teenager takes a photograph of graffiti.

OPPOSITE BELOW RIGHT: Emoticons— smiley faces for text messages.

morals. *Tom Jones*, *Moll Flanders,* and *Fanny Hill* caused furrowed brows. Novels were unsuitable for the masses! There was no religious redemption for the delinquents — Moll Flanders gets money, not morals!

With increased literacy, alphabets triumphed, but the fascination with symbolism did not die. When old symbols were discarded, they were re-used. The creation of "imaginary communities" such as nations, ethnic groups, communities, and esoteric and religious organizations recycled discarded symbols as part of the history and identity of their group.

Are symbols always meaningful? Umberto Eco was asked why he had entitled his novel *The Name of the Rose.* His answer was that the symbol of the

rose was so rich in meanings that by now it hasn't any meaning. And it disoriented the reader who was allowed to choose any one interpretation. Thus, a symbol only means what the reader sees in it.

Mundane symbols fill our world. A traveler can find a toilet or phone without using any language. Our streets and clothes are cluttered with logos. Our food arrives in packets with company symbols. As we buy it, it is scanned using barcode symbols, and going home, public transportation is covered in tags and graffiti. We have emoticons for email and text messages. Symbolism lives.

CHAPTER ONE
SYMBOLISM IN ART &
THE INVENTION OF TRADITION

THE POOR MAN'S BIBLE
Until the 19th century, few people were
literate and the church used illustrative
material to teach moral lessons,
explaining good and evil and the
consequences of sin. Christian art began
in the catacombs of Rome, with a very
simple young Christ as the good
shepherd. Early Christian art symbolized
a minority cult. In Byzantium it became
a state religion and the mood changed.
Mosaics in Aya Sofia, Istanbul, and
Rome depict not only biblical characters
but also emperors and empresses
symbolizing the state sanction of the
religion. Christ becomes Christ
Pantocrator — the ruler of all.

*RIGHT: Christ appears powerful in
Byzantium.*

*OPPOSITE: Modern Indian stained glass
shows the all-seeing eye of judgment.*

Craftsmen exercised their arts on the doors, chancels, ceiling bosses, walls, and windows of cathedrals. Everything was in glorious color. It was usual to have carvings on the west front, and often these showed the last judgment, leaving viewers in no doubts as to what awaits the souls of sinners and righteous men.

Angels with trumpets announce the resurrection and the dead rise from their graves. Christ appears at the second coming, seated on a rainbow or throne and surrounded by a mandorla of light, as the judge of mankind. The apostles sit on either side, distinguishable by personal symbols. Dives, a rich man who ignored Lazarus in his poverty, is in hell. Lazarus is comforted in Abraham's bosom. Dives begs Lazarus for water.

In some paintings, the Virgin and St. John intercede for the judged. The choirs of the elect are on the clouds, and below are the scales for the weighing of souls, administered by the angels. Adam and Eve prostrate themselves in prayer. A fiery stream leading to a lake of fire descends on the left. On the other side, the souls of the blessed are in paradise. These symbols combined must have struck fear into the hearts of common sinners.

Another popular lesson was the seven deadly sins. Pride is the most deadly and is frequently shown with a mirror. "Pride comes before a fall," and pride caused the fall of Lucifer. Anger is symbolized as a man with a whip, to lash out and to flagellate himself;

Gluttony with his huge belly shows the evil effect on body and soul; Avarice descends to hell clutching his money bags. Sloth, inattention to spiritual duty, is symbolized by someone asleep at prayers, or a priest dozing, rosary on the floor. Envy is often in green and eaten up by his own

BELOW: The souls are weighed and the devils await.

OPPOSITE: The centaur symbolizes two parts of the soul, and the dual nature of man and beast.

cravings. Lust is shown as an embrace, sometimes with a money bag. Horrid punishments await all.

A tree is often used to symbolize the sins, with pride at the top. *The Canterbury Tales* (1387–1400) described the sins and their opposing virtues. Chaucer saw the sin as the trunk and deadly branches and the fruit as human suffering, a tree of death.

RENAISSANCE ART

During the Renaissance, art changed. Under the Medicis, artists such as Botticelli, Fillippo Lippi, Leonardo da Vinci, Ghirlandaio, and Michelangelo were producing masterpieces in Florence.

These masters still painted religious works, but now artists had to please patrons and a taste for the classical world, myth, and allegory entered art.

In *Pallas and the Centaur*, Botticelli showed a wild creature brought under control by Pallas Athena. Virtue conquers sensuality.

Primavera, the allegory of spring, is interpreted in various ways. Certainly, Mercury, revealer of the truth is on the left, with the three Graces dancing next to him. Venus is in

the center and on the right, the fleeing nymph, Chloris is transformed into Flora, goddess of Spring, by Zephyrus, god of the West Winds. As "small print," there are hundreds of symbolic plants and flowers.

Some think the painting represents Lorenzo's political alliances with Italian city-states. Florence is represented by Flora, and the cupid, symbol of passionate love, is named Amor, an anagram of Roma (Rome). The other characters relate to Naples, Venice, Genoa, Pisa, and so on.

Botticelli also painted *The Birth of Venus*, about which the scholar E. H. Gombrich commented that Venus does not represent lust, but "love and charity, dignity and magnanimity, liberality and magnificence, comeliness and modesty, charm and splendour." A secular, mythical symbolism emerged in Botticelli's use of allegory, but it was acceptable to the eyes of Christians of the day.

The artistic movements that followed were founded on this art.

OPPOSITE: Botticelli painted Venus, the goddess of Love, in several well-known paintings.

OPPOSITE RIGHT: The altar of the Church of St. Nicholas, showing the Virgin Mary, Baroque arch and oil painting with gold statues.

Baroque saw a return to spirituality and tradition; Rococo was sensuous and joyful with mythical figures, goddesses, and cupids in landscapes. Romanticism expressed beauty and emotion and, in William Blake, a reflection of the symbolism of the day. Neo-classicism sought a revival of the ideals of classical Greece and Rome. The Pre-Raphaelite Brotherhood's paintings were noble, medieval, and rich with symbolism.

THE SYMBOLISTS

Symbolism developed from poetry. Baudelaire believed that meaning was also conveyed through the sound and rhythm of words. The movement, active in all the arts, produced a manifesto in 1886.

Symbolist art came from the imagination, fantasy, and the private world of the self. Artists were not

LEFT: In 1888 Van Gogh produced several paintings of sunflowers, some of the most popular paintings ever. They are intense but joyful and symbolize the brevity of life, from full bloom to withered and wilted.

OPPOSITE LEFT: Picasso took art in new directions. He enjoyed using clay and producing ceramics with paintings. His subjects were often fish and birds, as here in his rooster vase.

OPPOSITE RIGHT: A mural in Shankill Road, Belfast, Northern Ireland, a Protestant area, showing clenched fists and the Red Hand of Ulster.

painting what they saw but looking within. The focus of art tended toward dreams, mysticism, the erotic, debauchery, and death. The artists aimed to evoke emotion through their use of color and line. The movement was the ancestor of abstract art.

If artists used traditional symbolism and allegory, it was adapted to modern themes: Marcel Duchamp gave the *Mona Lisa* a mustache and Warhol's most celebrated symbols are of consumerism —Campbell's soup and Marilyn Monroe.

Kenneth Clark observed, "Fifty years ago we were told that the subjects of pictures were of no importance; all

INVENTION OF TRADITION

The historian Eric Hobsbawm wrote: "'Invented tradition' is taken to mean a set of practices, normally governed by overtly or tacitly accepted rules of a ritual or symbolic nature, which seek to inculcate certain values and norms of behaviour by repetition, which automatically implies continuity with the past. In fact, where possible, they normally attempt to establish continuity with a suitable historic past … However, insofar as there is such reference to a historic past, the peculiarity of 'invented' traditions is that the continuity with it is largely fictitious. In short, they are responses to novel situations which take the form of reference to old situations, or which establish their own past by quasi-obligatory repetition."

Particularly evident in the last 200 years, this "invention" led to an immense change in the use of symbols, by

that mattered was the form and color. This was a curious aberration of criticism, because all artists, from the cave painters onwards, had attached great importance to their subject matter. Giotto, Bellini, Titian, Michelangelo, Poussin, or Rembrandt would have thought it incredible that such a doctrine could gain currency."

It is telling that we have lost the art of reading symbolism in paintings and buildings. It is now something that has to be learned.

nations, communities, ethnic groups, and esoteric societies.

In an area as small as the British Isles, various identities were invented.

ULSTER LOYALIST SYMBOLS

Most symbols are religious or historical. King Billy (William III of Orange) appears in murals accompanied by symbols of Protestantism: the open Bible, or a Star of David (Ulster Protestants related to a persecuted lost tribe of Israel; and the six points can also be seen as representing the Six Counties). The clenched fist, surrounded by barbed

BELOW: IRA mural on Falls Road, Belfast, Northern Ireland.

OPPOSITE: This mural on the Falls Road uses a chained fist.

wire says, "Our only crime is loyalty". Loyalists use British symbols, the

crown and flags.

Acronyms (UDA, the Ulster Defence Association), dates (1690, the Battle of the Boyne) and slogans ("No surrender") are common.

At annual parades, Orangemen appear in their best suits and orange sashes. The sashes bear the insignia of the Lodge, symbols of their historic heritage. The bowler hats perhaps once symbolized authority, but as bowler hats become rare, fewer are worn.

NATIONALIST SYMBOLS

The symbolic color for Irish Catholics is green: the wearing of the green is associated with the St. Patrick's Day parade, a custom begun in New York in 1762. The shamrock, held to be a sacred plant of the Celts, is worn. In the 17th century it became a symbol of Irish nationalism.

Nationalist symbolism is shown in murals featuring the Irish tricolor, harps, shamrocks, the crest of Celtic Football Club, and symbols of the local area. Symbolic acronyms, such as "IRA," and dates, such as "1916," also feature.

One symbol crossed traditions but is now perhaps more associated with the Loyalists and Unionists: the Red Hand of Ulster, the flag of the province.

SYMBOLISM IN ART & THE INVENTION OF TRADITION

RIGHT: Until the 18th century, the most common symbol of Welsh identity was the three ostrich feathers of the Prince of Wales. These still appear on Welsh rugby shirts.

BELOW RIGHT: The daffodil, another symbol of Wales.

SCOTTISH SYMBOLS

Braveheart stirred emotions, but is not noted for historical accuracy. The people it portrays simply didn't have kilts. They wore a plaid, which was not necessarily a plaid in the sense accepted in North America. The word meant a large wrap, about five yards long (4.6 meters) and 60 inches (152 centimeters) wide. It was wrapped and possibly belted around the body, but not sewn into pleats. In 1746, after Culloden, symbols of Gaelic Scottishness were banned and the clan system broke down. After 35 years, the act was repealed and it was then that "clan tartans" relating to no longer viable clans appeared. Much tradition is traceable to one man—Sir Walter Scott.

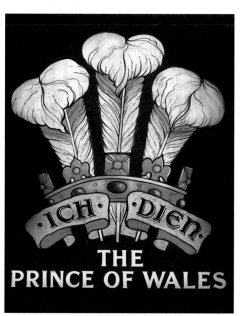

THE
PRINCE OF WALES

The kilt, which some claim was an invention of an Englishman, Thomas Rawlinson, appeared in the 18th century, and canny shopkeepers were quick to provide "family tartans." Today, a greenish tartan symbolizes the Pakistani homeland of the Khan family who settled in Scotland.

WELSH SYMBOLS

The Welsh in London and America had St. David's Day processions from 1714, going to church wearing leeks on their hats. The origin of the leek as a symbol is said to be a battle that took place in a field of leeks, in which the Welsh were ordered to put leeks on their helmets for recognition. Shakespeare, in the 16th century, viewed the leek as an ancient tradition: his Henry V wears a leek and says, "I am Welsh, you know, good countryman." The use of the daffodil dates from 1907 and is thought to come from a misunderstanding of the Welsh word for bulb, meaning both the leek and the daffodil flower.

In the 18th century, the Welsh "rediscovered" Celts and Druids. Iolo Morgannwg, stonemason and artist, manufactured many symbols. The best known is the *nod cyfrin*, or awen, a sign with three bars symbolizing past, present, and future, representing God.

DRUIDS

Druids performed ceremonies in Iron Age pre-Christian Western Europe. They were polytheists and venerated the sun, sky, land, sacred trees, and groves. They followed the seasons, and their festivals are the ones now used by Wicca. They showed particular devotion to the oak, hazel, and mistletoe. Several divinities were symbolized by fire, a cleansing medium.

In the 18th century, John Aubrey, who was fascinated by megalithic monuments, made a connection between Stonehenge and druids, but had no authority for making this claim. The British Museum states that "there is no link between Iron Age druids and Stonehenge." The monument's builders and users were not druids, and had vanished before the Iron Age.

LEFT: Stonehenge —the monument's builders had vanished before the druids appeared.

OPPOSITE ABOVE: Druids salute the sun.

OPPOSITE BELOW: Urdu became the "mother tongue" of Pakistan, and a powerful symbol for Muslims.

However, romantic notions pay little heed to scholars (and vice versa). Neo-druids have reclaimed Stonehenge with their robes and ceremonies.

Ancient druidic symbols are unknown, apart from the sun wheel with its six or eight spokes. It is considered a representation of the solar calendar, and the inspiration for the Celtic cross. One interpretation of Stonehenge is as a calendar. The best-known druidic symbol is the sigil used by the Reformed Druids of North America, dating from the 1960s. It is a circle with two vertical lines running through it. It may be decorated with oak leaves.

PRIEURÉ DE SION

An amusing invention is the *Prieuré de Sion*, a hoax perpetrated by Pierre Plantard in 1956. Plantard was a pretender to the French throne and wanted an organization with a thousand years of "History" to support his claims. The symbol of the organization is a fleur de lys, with some loops and triangles. Plantard's hoax is central to the plot of *The Da Vinci Code*.

AFRICA AND INDIA

"Traditions" have not only been invented in Europe. In Africa "tribes" were given their own traditions, in which identity symbols were invented and, astonishingly, accepted. This has led to appalling strife.

In India, Hinduism, Sikhism, Islam and other religions underwent "revival." The religions were being "returned" to their pristine past: back to the Vedas, the Prophet, and the Guru. Language was made a symbol of identity, Hindus adhering to Hindi and Devanagari script, Sikhs to Panjabi and Gurmukhi script, and Muslims choosing Urdu and Persian script. Even the way one greets someone in the street is radically different! The resulting mixture of

religion and nationalism has led to inter-religious strife.

Each group adopted external identity markers, of which the Sikh "five Ks" are especially striking. These items each begin with the letter K in Panjabi: uncut hair — *kesh*; comb — *kanga*; special shorts — *kacha*; bangle — *kara*; and dagger — *kirpan*. To these has been added the turban.

Hindus have huge numbers of symbols relating to caste, belief, sect, and region. The most important symbol is the Aum, the primal syllable first mentioned in the Upanishads and an important symbol of Hinduism.

Inventing tradition meant finding universal symbols that had to be basic to avoid disagreement and misunderstanding. Recently, Hundutva (Hinduness), the Hindu fundamentalists, have stressed the

LEFT: Sikhs are unmistakable in their turbans.

OPPOSITE LEFT: The Aum is the prime symbol of Hinduism.

OPPOSITE RIGHT: The River Ganges as a goddess, springing from Siva's hair and riding a crocodile.

symbols of the sacred cow (anti-cow slaughter); Mother India; and the River Ganges. Hindu military figures of the past are also used.

Neo-Hinduism was the creation of a western-educated elite who drew ideas and symbols from all religious traditions. They had no problem with Annie Besant, who took over as leader of the Theosophists in India when Madame Blavatsky (see p53) died in 1891. Although Besant and the Neo-Hindus had both differences and shared ideals, they sustained the Indian National Congress and the nationalist movement that brought India to independence.

CHAPTER TWO
ALCHEMY, MAGIC & RITUALS

Hermes, the Greek messenger of the gods, also called Hermes Trismegistus, is claimed as the god who introduced alchemy and magic. "Hermetic" has come to mean secret and hidden traditions.

Alchemy was part of Greek and Roman learning: Plato's Academy, where

philosophy, mathematics, logic, and science were important subjects of research, dates from 385 BCE. The Academy's tradition continued until it was closed by the Emperor Justinian in 529 CE. Closure led to the dispersal of

ABOVE: Alchemist in his laboratory.

LEFT: Hermes at Syros, Greece.

OPPOSITE: An alchemist, painted in 1661.

LEFT: The alchemist Avicenna (Abu Ali Al Hosain Ibn Sina), the Master of Alchemy. From Michael Maier, Symbola aurea mensae duodecim nationum, *1617.*

BELOW: To transmute base metals into gold — an alchemist's quest.

OPPOSITE LEFT: A bishop raising the host during mass.

OPPOSITE RIGHT: The Emerald Tablet of Hermes Trismegistus.

stoves), and soap.

Alchemy was important in India and China. In China they worked with gold, jade, and cinnabar and poisonous scholars and their texts to Islamic lands where the knowledge was valued and expanded. Eventually, this learning returned to Europe.

Muslim scholars used scientific, experimental methods, and developed theories. Critical scholars such as Al Biruni and Ibn Sina discredited various ideas in alchemy and astrology. This phase produced scientific advance and regularized some processes such as distillation and filtration to make medicines, perfumes, kerosene (for

essential to achieving all goals. The stone would give immense power and aid mystic philosophical speculation, enabling man to reach perfection, like gold. Mutability was the basis of human expectation in those days. Whatever it was, it could change. Grain could be transmuted into bread and grapes into wine. Bread and wine transubstantiated into the body and blood of Christ, so alchemy was not incompatible with religion. Man could be transmuted from his short life of sickness and his evil

ways to perfection — healthy and with everlasting life.

THE EMERALD TABLET

An early text concerning these goals of alchemy, the Emerald or Smaragdina Tablet, is said to come from Hermes Trismegistus. The oldest known source of the tablet is the *Kitab Sirr al Asrar* written by Jilani in *c*.800 CE. After the tablet was returned to Europe it was a major influence in medieval and renaissance alchemy. It was greatly

mercury, sulfur, and arsenic. Alchemy was similar in different countries; perhaps it passed from one culture to another. Expertise came to Europe through Arabic translations and writings in classical languages. This explains, for example, why Na is the symbol for sodium (Latin *natrium*) and K for potassium (*kalium*).

Alchemists sought to transmute base metals into gold, but the true search of alchemy was spiritual. They sought an elixir of life that would cure all ills and prolong life. And they sought the philosopher's stone, believed

LEFT: The Rosicrucians' symbolic representation of the Emerald Tablet in 1875.

OPPOSITE LEFT: St. Thomas Aquinas contemplated the question of whether alchemical gold could be sold as real: as long as it had all the properties of gold, he viewed it permissible.

OPPOSITE RIGHT: Roger Bacon.

valued, and translated by Newton, Bacon, Maier, Albertus Magnus, and Crowley.

Rosicrucians (see p49) published a symbolic representation of the Emerald Tablet in 1875. A circle, symbolizing oneness and unity, surrounds the tablet. The words' initial letters spell out the secret of alchemy, VITRIOL: Visita—visit; Interiora — the interior; Terrae – earth; Rectificando — in rectifying; Invenies — discover; Occultum — occult; Lapidem — stone.

The hands symbolize an oath and the polarity of our being, the duality of which must be united in "chemical marriage."

Above the hands are the seven planets; the sun and moon pour life substance into a chalice, thus uniting opposite natures. The chalice is supported by Mercury, which is both male and female and another union of opposites.

The great work consists of the union of the sun and moon with the aid of Mercury.

To the left are Mars and Saturn, and to the right, Venus and Jupiter, and the planets are thus balanced and polarized.

The three shields are the three principles; sulfur is the lion; salt, the seven-pointed star; and Mercury, the eagle. Mercury in alchemy and Mercury in astrology are related but not the same. The chalice symbolizes water; the lion, fire; the eagle, air; and the star, earth.

the star is the alchemical symbol for vitriol. On the opposite side of the ring from Mercury, the stone arises from the conjunction of these two.

There are two spheres symbolizing heaven and earth. In the very center is a ring, the circle of the macrocosm and microcosm. Below the ring and above

Each of these symbols and their conjunction has a wealth of meaning for those versed in alchemy. The tablet was used for meditation and visualization. It is said to contain the method to produce alchemical gold and to bring consciousness to a very high level.

MEDIEVAL ALCHEMISTS

St. Albertus Magnus (1206–80), a Dominican, introduced Greek and Arabic science back into Europe. He was a greatly respected scholar and conducted experiments in biological and medical science — forays into alchemy. He used stones and herbs for medical and moral ends: The immortal soul was the most important.

Roger Bacon (1214–94) is considered to have been a stickler for experimental methods. To be worthwhile, a procedure needed to be demonstrated in the laboratory and confirmed by scientific demonstration. Alchemy now had a firm intellectual base.

AL-ANDALUS

Classical and Islamic learning arrived in Europe through Al-Andalus, Moorish Spain. Spain was ruled by the Muslims at various times between 711 and 1492. The Moors had enormous libraries that included works from classical times that had already been translated into Arabic. They read voraciously and their love of calligraphy produced works of great beauty. Among the books that came to Europe via this route were grimoires. The libraries were destroyed by the Spanish inquisition in the 16th century.

GRIMOIRES

To the modern reader, grimoires usually refer to computer and fantasy games. Originally, a grimoire was a "grammar," a book of instructions, mainly produced between the 13th and 15th centuries and written by devout Christians. Most grimoires are largely not about pacts with the devil; they are more likely to feature biblical references. Grimoires contain much information about guardian angels and their teachings.

Grimoires also offer spells and charms, lotions and potions, and talismans. Users were keen on finding treasure, flying, becoming invisible, and influencing the course of love affairs. Extremely lengthy rituals were recorded, lasting for months, to enable adepts aided by angels to conjure

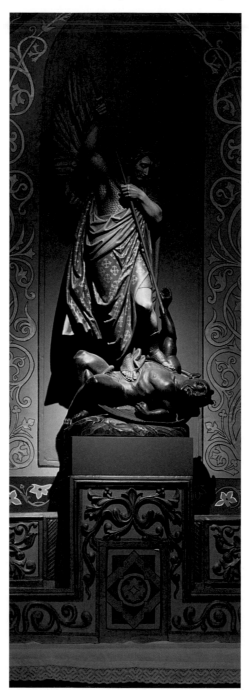

LEFT: The Archangel Michael slays the devil, Abbaye de St. Michel de Frigolet, Provence, France.

OPPOSITE: Herbs are prepared with a pestle and mortar.

spirits and demons. Signs representing the true names of angels and demons were necessary to grant the practitioner a measure of control over them. To this day, many books reproduce numbers of them, often with no explanation. Sigils are used in modern magic, but users often form their own unique ideas into special sigils that are charged with power.

Ceremonial magic required purification and preparation. Ceremonial robes were worn, and the practitioner needed proper protection with symbols, protective amulets, and talismans. Assistants also required symbols on their clothing and equipment.

Various knives, swords, wands, chalices, candles, salt and wine, were required, and water and herbs were prepared in containers.

Chalk was needed to draw circles, triangles and other shapes. The practitioner's protection was a circle, and any demons conjured were

contained in a triangle. Once the symbols were drawn it was believed that they had their own power. Magic circles were vital and were inscribed on parchment or engraved on a precious metal. A circle contained triangles, or five- or six-pointed stars, and within these geometric shapes Hebrew letters, cabalistic signs, and Latin words were written. These symbols were believed to trap and control occult powers. Medieval grimoires like *The Key of Solomon* offer many patterns.

In medieval times stars were used by Christians and alchemists. The six-pointed star's triangles symbolized fire and water and, therefore, transmutation. The five-pointed star symbolized the five elements (earth, fire, water, air, and spirit), or Christ's five wounds. The current associations of the symbols come much later in history.

The practitioner of magic might use an ancient grimoire or produce a "Book of Shadows" of his own designing.

RENAISSANCE FLORENCE

Cosimo de Medici (1389–1464) brought classical learning home. In 1439 Cosimo's Neo-Platonic academy was established in Florence. Marcilio Ficino, a highly intelligent youth, was educated in Greek philosophy and translated classics including Homer and Hermes Trismegistus. Apart from the classics, Ficino was influenced by a grimoire called the *Picatrix*.

The Neo-Platonists sought to merge Platonic and Neo-Platonic ideas with Christian thought, planning to regenerate freedom of intellect as they imagined it had been in classical times. This was to lead to the development of humanism: the idea that man had a right to use his own powers of reasoning and beliefs,

and that an individual could use the power of learning and science to make himself whole.

Elsewhere in Europe, the richer classes were fascinated by anything new and exotic, hoping to benefit from efforts they sponsored. One surprising product of an alchemist for his master is Danziger Goldwasser, a strong liqueur

ABOVE: Containers of chemicals.

LEFT: Cosimo de Medici.

OPPOSITE LEFT: Goldwasser is a strong liqueur that has been produced since 1598.

OPPPOSITE RIGHT: Plate from the Mutus Liber.

of extracts and liquors, all spurred by alchemy.

THE SPREAD OF KNOWLEDGE

Cosimo had collected libraries of texts; his grandson Lorenzo the Magnificent had classical texts brought from the East. He had translations and copies made and circulated throughout Europe.

This produced what the scholar Frances A. Yates described as "a churning turbid flood of Hermetic, cabalistic, Gnostic, theurgic, Sabaean, Pythagorean, and generally mystic notions" that "broke over Europe carrying everything before it," and this led to a fascination with the occult, which continued unabated for several centuries.

ALCHEMISTS AND SYMBOLS —*Mutus Liber*

Symbols were a central part of alchemy. Pages of books were filled with symbolic illustrations. In one 17th-century French manual, the *Mutus Liber,* there is a wordless guide to producing the philosopher's stone.

On the left is the sun and a ram, and on the right, the moon and a bull. There are fabrics pegged out on frames and a couple are wringing liquid from a cloth into a container. A town in the background has several churches marked with crosses. Rays are falling onto the field.

The couple are collecting dew, which has settled on the fabric. Dew is an element needed for the philosopher's stone. The book makes reference to Genesis 27, v.28: "God gave thee of the dew of heaven and the fatness of earth, and plenty of corn and wine," a quotation that also appears in Dee's *Hieroglyphic Monad* (1564). The sun is the father and the moon the mother, while the bull and ram are Aries and

that has been produced since 1598. The name comes from the fact that there are small flakes of 22-carat gold suspended in the liquid, making it interesting and beautiful "medicine," for it was believed that to ingest gold was highly beneficial. The time of its appearance coincided with the height of alchemical investigations.

A German alchemist analyzed some white earth and discovered the secret of Chinese porcelain, and thus was launched Dresden porcelain. Over the centuries there were many advances in metalwork, inks, dyes, paints, ceramics, and glass, and the production

Taurus. So the time is specific — the sun is in Aries and the moon in Taurus. In Dee's monad, Aries and Taurus are joined by a cross. The rays from sun and moon are mixed. Further symbolism is embedded in the number of rays and crosses.

It has been claimed that symbolism was necessary to keep the knowledge hidden from authorities or common people. Probably more to the point, symbols were used to prevent rival practitioners for stealing ideas and gaining advantage.

The main reason for all the symbolism is that those who used it were obsessed with symbols, to a level almost incomprehensible today. This laborious effort of drawing some of these glyphs would have been time-consuming — but this is not a drawback if one believes that symbols are vital for rituals: drawing was part of the ritual. Also, the glyph, thought to summarize vast areas of human knowledge onto a

LEFT: Plate Two from the Mutus Liber.

OPPOSITE LEFT: John Dee.

OPPOSITE RIGHT: Page from John Dee's Hieroglyphic Monad.

to the "intellectual furniture" of the time in which they were produced. A man has ideas, beliefs, notions, and a culture of his own age and society, and men used combinations of symbols to encapsulate knowledge.

JOHN DEE'S *MONAD*

John Dee (1527–1608) was adviser and "noble intelligencer" to Elizabeth I. He was interested in astrology, cartography, medicine, and alchemy, and given to conversation with angels. Dee and Sir Edward Kelley claimed the "Enochian" alphabet and language was given to them by angels — it was used in Enochian magic and to evoke angels. Enoch was a Biblical character, an ancestor of Noah and Methuselah, believed to have become an angel in old age. He is said to have interceded for fallen angels.

Dee's *Monad* was produced in 1564. His mind, "pregnant for seven years," delivered in twelve days. It consists of the symbols for Mercury and for Aries (a fire sign, and the first sign of the Zodiac). Mercury and fire are of major importance in alchemy.

The upper part of the symbol shows the sun and moon moving around the earth, the point in the center of the

single page. There was a belief that symbols of themselves held magic power. For whatever reason, accuracy was vital.

Paracelsus, the Swiss alchemist, believed that signs, characters, and letters had force and efficacy, and were best used harmonized with the forces of the cosmos. Letters could be used for practical purposes, like healing.

Successive scholars produced new symbols of their own designing. These symbols were personal and conformed

circle. The cross represents Christianity, with the four elements indicated by the lines, a numerical aspect to the symbol. Dee was a Christian and believed that God's creation was number-based. The importance of numbers also came from Platonic thought and the harmonics of Pythagoras, mathematical proportions, and the Bible. Dee believed the *Monad* was the key to understanding the unity of the cosmos.

MICHAEL MAIER: SQUARING THE CIRCLE

Michael Maier (1558–1622) met Dee in Prague and was initiated into the wisdom Dee had harvested.

The master points his compass from a circle to a circle (or square to circle), and demonstrates the squaring of the circle, symbolic of the marriage of heaven and earth:

Around the man and woman draw a ring,
From which an equal sided square springs forth.
From this derive a triangle, which should touch
The sphere on every side: and then the Stone
Will have arisen. If this is not clear, Then Learn Geometry, and know it all.

The man and woman are opposed symbols, they are one but also two, and added, make three. In a multiplicity they make four, and then return to one. The largest circle shows spiritual, all-encompassing love. Spheres within spheres show a recipe for the elixir, the Philosopher's stone.

LEFT: Michael Maier.

ABOVE: Squaring the circle.

OPPOSITE LEFT: Cornelius Agrippa von Nettesheim.

OPPOSITE RIGHT: Alphabet from Cornelius Agrippa, De Occulta Philosophia, *1533 edition.*

CORNELIUS AGRIPPA VON NETTESHEIM AND ALPHABETS

Scholars didn't know what to make of the controversial works of Agrippa von Nettesheim — Cornelius Agrippa (1486–1535). There are works attributed to him that he didn't write, complicating the issue. Some readers of his works hoped to gain magic and alchemical secrets. Some thought he was being satirical, and others thought that he was denouncing society for corruption, injustice, and hypocrisy.

He had a desire to reclaim classical learning and hoped for a renewal of religion, society, and justice with wisdom based on Renaissance humanism, the Bible, and sages of old, but cleansed of errors. He thought that science had degenerated, and that a mixture of neo-classical learning, Hermetic philosophy, cabala, and Christianity were the remedy.

Agrippa's universe was tripartite, the lowest level being the elemental, material world; second was a celestial level of astrological and mathematical

matters ruled by planets; and the highest, intellectual level was the realm of angels and demons, good and bad intelligences. The whole was ruled over by God. The four elements, earth, air, fire, and water, played a role at all levels, but there are things that are not understood at all: these are accounted for by a world spirit — the fifth element. Agrippa believed that various symbols, letters, words, numerals, and images could express relations between these worlds and, as the symbols carried the power of the beings they represented, the symbols could be used to affect the natural world.

AGRIPPA AND ALPHABETS

In pursuit of symbols with power to affect the natural world, Agrippa placed great importance on Hebrew letters, because he believed that the symbols and powers were best expressed by Jewish cabalists. Hebrew was believed to be the original language given to Adam by God, so it was charged with the strongest magic power. Words, letters, and numbers are symbols that have an intrinsic, essential relationship with that which they represent.

Hebrew letters also denote

numbers, and it is possible to calculate numbers with mystic power from sacred texts, enabling tables, and magic squares to be prepared. The squares represent planetary powers.

Geometric figures could also be part of the equation: the circle represented one and the pentagon five. These could be added with Hebrew letters to make something significant.

ABOVE: An Eliphas Lévi pentagram with an assortment of letters and symbols.

RIGHT: A modern interpretation of hieroglyphs — write your own name.

OPPOSITE: Hieroglyphs on a temple at Luxor, Egypt.

Further study enables words to be derived — names deriving power from the numbers.

Manipulating letters and numbers from the Hebrew texts meant that the names of Angels and Demons could be established. And as the names were true representations, power could be gained over them so that they could be controlled and made to do as they were bid.

Lists of the names of Angels and Demons, and even names of God, appeared. Symbols for these had been available from grimoires.

Agrippa was also responsible for the Angelic, Malachim, and Passing the River alphabets. The angelic alphabet was for communication with Angels. The parentage of the Malachim and Angelic alphabets is Greek and Hebrew scripts. "Passing the river" refers to the crossing of the Euphrates by Jews returning from exile in Babylon. The Theban alphabet is of unknown origin and is often called runic, though it has little in common with runes. First published in 1518, it was part of Agrippa's collection.

Egyptian hieroglyphs were seen as symbols from Hermes himself.

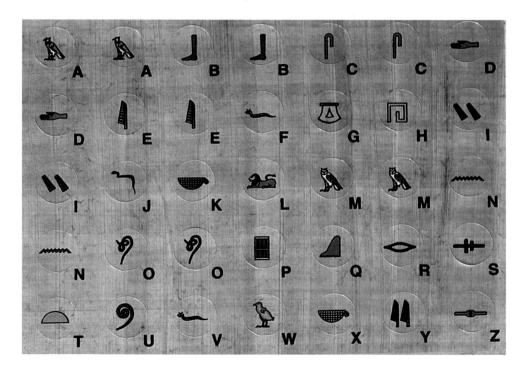

Although unable to interpret Egyptian hieroglyphs, scholars were fascinated by the idea of them. Athanasius Kirchner attempted to interpret them in 1633. Perhaps he interpreted them to his own satisfaction. Genuine interpretation was not possible until after the Rosetta Stone was found in 1799.

Hieroglyphs were prized because, from early times, it was said that Egyptians and other ancient people used a demotic alphabetic script, but that the sacred symbols were accessible only to the elite. In fact, the cognoscenti's use of symbolism appealed to their sense of hierarchy: those in the know had their own entrée to a world of mystery not open to common people. It was below their dignity to use ordinary, straightforward alphabets.

There were conflicting opinions as to the original language of paradise. Johannes Goropius, a resident of what is now Belgium, believed that Brabantia (Flemish from Antwerp) was the original one. He wasn't alone; the polymath Leibniz thought he might have discovered something of significance.

Although most of Agrippa's symbols are forgotten, those for the Zodiac, the seven planets, and seven alchemical substances remain recognizable. He also designed a symbolic man in a circle, very similar to Leonardo's Vitruvian man.

In concentrating on Jewish writings and cabala, Agrippa was not alone. In Renaissance Florence Cabala became an enthusiasm, leading to the emergence of Hermetic interpretations of Cabala.

CABALA

Enthusiasm for the Cabala spread across Europe. Here was a great source of hidden wisdom and not only the mystical significance of the letters was sought; even the punctuation was subject to calculation, and layers of secret truth were discovered in the Torah.

The Cabala interprets the essence of the Almighty as ten spheres or sephiroth, meaning emanations or levels of creation, ways in which God is revealed. He does not change, but the perception does. Each sephiroth must be passed in order to know the divine. The Cabala must be understood thoroughly before the human being can reach the tenth and highest level.

It is said that most people are ignorant of this knowledge, not following the discipline, but the individual can

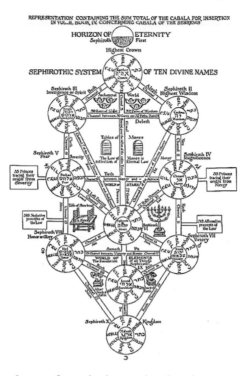

advance from the lowest level and progress upward.

This path is similar to the discipline of Sufism.

The sephiroth are arranged as a tree of life. The ten spheres are interconnected to represent the system of the ancient Cabalistic tradition. It is a symbolic map of the cosmos and lays out the path to enlightenment.

The circles represent the ten levels. Twenty-two channels, representing the letters of the Hebrew alphabet, connect them. The levels and letters have provided a rich source of mysticism.

ROBERT FLUDD

Robert Fludd (1574–1637), an occult philosopher, was influenced by Dee. Fludd believed in an interdependent macrocosm (the cosmos) and microcosm (mankind).

The frontispiece of his book shows man at the center. The circles indicate the four humours, planets, and the zodiac. The celestial spheres are also shown. There are many clouds, and a cord wrapped four times around the whole is pulled by a mythical creature with wings and hooves. It has an hourglass on its head. Fludd usually shows the universe in circles, like a

spiral of eternity and time.

Fludd produced many diagrams. One shows the divinatory sciences of

importance: prophecy, geomancy, the art of memory, the interpretation of horoscopes, physiognomy, palmistry, and the "science of pyramids." The last was Fludd's own idea. The whole picks up the macrocosm/microcosm of spiritual and material qualities.

Fludd had original ideas. He posited the idea of the circulation of the blood, and although his explanation was not correct — he thought that the blood circulated around the heart as spheres and planets revolve — Harvey kindly referred to it when he published a more accurate theory.

Fludd's symbolism became ever more complex as he attempted to reduce vast amounts of information into diagrams. He tabulated how heaven, man, and earth relate to musical theory. He also made a diagram showing how man links to the cosmos.

MEMORY SYSTEMS

Fludd, in common with others of his era, shared an interest in memory systems.

Memory systems had been used in classical times. When literacy was uncommon, people developed other methods of forming images and remembering information. It

was part of the Greek education system, so classical orators had no problem in speaking without a single note.

Ramon Llull (1232–1315) developed a memory system that could be used to "discover truth." He believed that a limited number of undeniable truths existed, and that a wheel of moving concentric circles marked with figures and letters could make combinations of concepts, generating logical proof.

Fludd believed that memories for storage could be transmuted into visual and spatial images. Our forebears used architectural features as symbols, speech-notes, and clues, an art that declined once print had become common. Architecture or memory wheels were used by many to aid recollection.

Churches and cathedrals have features like rose windows, which were certainly used as *aide-memoires*. The early Tarot cards were also used as a memory system, and the wheel of fortune was particularly useful.

The idea of memory systems is coming back into fashion in some circles. Visualizing ideas and relating them to places and objects prompts

memories. It often seems that memory is much better among the illiterate than the literate: the illiterate have to find ways other than lists to remember things.

The use of a "theater of memory" was suggested by Guido Camillo (1480–1544). The user visualizes himself on the stage and retrieves memories from the auditorium. The auditorium reflects the divine world in proportion to architectural images. The

LEFT: Ramon Llull is a popular subject for art in his homeland, Mallorca.

ABOVE: The Wheel of Fortune from the Tarot was used as a memory system.

OPPOSITE: Jacob Böhme.

mnemonic potential of a theater was also recognized by Palladio, whose Teatro Olympico at Vicenza was full of symbolic objects that could be used to aid memory.

It has been claimed (and disputed) that Fludd's system was based on the Globe, the Tudor theater in London where Shakespeare's plays were performed.

JACOB BÖHME

A change in direction came with the ideas of Jacob Böhme (1575–1624). He was a German Protestant mystic and shoemaker. Men like Böhme show that although the elite had tried to keep their ideas from the masses, the masses could turn their learning to undermine and challenge the elite. Ideas roughly based on Cabala were turned against the crushing contemporary interpretations of scripture that were stultifying Christian teaching. Böhme had a personal interpretation of the Bible based on the premise that great learning was not needed but that divine inspiration was vital. The relatively uneducated could do as well as the scholars who claimed authority to interpret scripture.

Böhme had visions and conversations with angels. He created

a symbol that he called the eye of God in the form of the letter "A," the first letter of the alphabet and related to the number 1. It is also the first letter of the word *Auge*, German for "eye." The symbol is made by placing an upturned A beneath the first A, as if reflected. The two together produce an eye shape and symbolize Böhme's belief that the creation is God's attempt to see himself. He makes an image and a reflection of himself so that he can see himself.

Dionysius Andreas Freher, an alchemist living in London, was inspired by Böhme, and produced 153 figures in a work called the *Paradoxical Emblems*. It began with a completely

blank page, symbolizing that "The Centre of Centres is everywhere, the Circumference nowhere."

The following page has a single dot signifying "This point rests in itself, is sufficient for itself; wants Nothing and Contains all Things." The symbolism becomes increasingly complex until the conclusion is reached — "All Things were, are, and will be. Out of One, Through One, and to One."

Böhme's influence was enormous. The religious William Law observed, "Words were made to mean what they have never meant before and have never meant since." Law's mystical ideas set him apart from old friends like John and Charles Wesley, who were more practical. William Blake owes much to Böhme and to Paracelsus. He developed ideas of prophecy in art from studying their works.

Sir Isaac Newton (1642–1727) is known as probably the most influential scientist of all time, noted for his ideas on gravity, the laws of motion, and his work on optics and calculus. He spent more time on alchemy than he did on physics and optics. Newton was interested in finding out how metals were formed in nature.

The Beginning of the End

Böhme desired to undermine the power of the elite. He exchanged ideas on Hermetic and scientific approaches with Johannes Kepler. The reality was that many upcoming young scholars no longer accepted hermetical ideas and magical thinking as useful.

The great art historian E. M. Gombrich said that philosophers like Ficino sought a "super sensible" realm beyond the sensible world. Physical objects bore a symbolic relationship with metaphysical forms and, duplicating these symbols in hieroglyphic form, the philosopher could harmonize his own symbols to

RIGHT: Galileo argued in favor of a sun-centered universe and clear unambiguous writing.

OPPOSITE RIGHT: Armillary spheres or spherical astrolobes used rings to represent the principal circles of heaven. They were developed by Muslims in the Middle Ages and come in Ptolemaic models, with earth at the center, or Copernican, with everything revolving around the sun.

OPPOSITE LEFT: Sir Isaac Newton.

"the cosmic network of affinities and correspondences."

Gombrich noted that interest in symbols waned as people became more literate. When merchants and others could read, the hierarchy was disrupted. The focus shifted toward openness and clarity — people wanted to be able to communicate effectively and with no possibility of error. The scholar was no longer respected as having special knowledge, and the notion that there were truths unsuitable for the common man was discredited. Gombrich also observed that little value was placed on clarity in Renaissance iconography and that symbols "seemed to become more

obscure the triter the meaning they were supposed to hide or reveal."

The world was changing. In 1543 Ptolemaic geocentric ideas were turned on their head when Copernicus wrote *On the Revolution of the Heavenly Spheres,* and replaced the old model with a heliocentric one. Ancient alchemists knew of only seven metals — gold, silver, copper, iron, tin, lead, and mercury. As time passed, other elements were added. The modern table of the elements would have pulled the rug from under the alchemists' feet. The only planets visible with the naked eye were Venus, Mercury, Mars, Saturn, and Jupiter, which were added to the sun and moon.

A debate opened in England concerning the teaching at Oxford and Cambridge, and the old ideas of occult science came up against the Royal Society's new materialist science. The Royal Society had begun meeting in the 1640s, was formally founded in 1660, and would become an independent scientific academy and a learned society. Robert Boyle (1627–91), who formulated Boyle's law, is considered the first real chemist. The author of *The Sceptical Chymist*, he wrote that matter consists of atoms and that all phenomena

are a result of collisions of atoms. He wanted "the Chymists Doctrine out of their Dark and Smoakie Laboratories and into the open light."

Openness and clarity won the day. Reformers like Bacon, Comenius, Galileo and others hailed clear writing using recognizable alphabets. These were seen as remarkably useful inventions. People would no longer try to pack huge amounts of information into a monad. Fascination with ancient scripts was gone. Knowledge was not to be obscured but to be made available to all men.

Henceforth, symbolism was to become a way to explain things — useful, but hardly magical.

INVENTING MAGICAL TRADITION
When modern sciences emerged, the baggage of traditional alchemy, astrology, cosmology, ceremonial magic, and hermetic philosophy was abandoned, but a few adherents set about inventing their own traditions. The past offered plenty of material.

What emerged was esotericism, the parent of new age philosophy. The actual word "esoteric" was older, originating from Greek and in use in English since 1655, but popularized by Eliphas Levi (see p50).

Almost all esoteric organizations claim great antiquity, or to have come from somewhere remote, or preferably both. Favored locations include Atlantis, Himalayan fastnesses, or cities under the surface of the earth. Inventors of such traditions are free to select — so everything can be explained and nothing is left unexplainable.

ROSICRUCIANISM
Controversy abounds as to the foundation of the Rosicrucians. Christian Rosencreuz was said to have

lived in the 14th century and to have left manifestos packed with symbolism discovered by German Protestants in the 17th century. He also left *The Chemical Wedding of Christian Rosenkreuz*, in which the marriage ceremony is used as a symbol for an initiation into alchemy.

The modern Rosicrucian movement, called AMORC (Ancient Mystical Order of Rosea Crucis), was founded in 1915 by Harvey Spencer Lewis. It promoted educational, mystic, and humanitarian values.

There is a Rosicrucian alphabet and many symbols. The Rosy Cross symbolizes the brotherhood. It symbolizes Christ's blood, and the seven-petalled flower on the cross represents the seven levels of initiation of the order. The rose at the center represents the heart of Christ, divine

light, and the sun at the center of the wheel of life. The Golden and Rosy Cross symbol is an insignia: it bears alchemical symbols for salt, sulfur, and mercury, a star, and the words "faith," "hope," "love," and "patience." Rosicrucians wish to transmute the base metal of ignorance to the pure gold of wisdom through an understanding of the rituals, and through the secrets of the brotherhood.

FREEMASONRY

The history of Freemasonry smacks of invented tradition, with claims of links to King Solomon, the Temple at Jerusalem, and many historic groups and events since that time. Evidence to link them to the medieval masons who built cathedrals is thin. This contrasts with the wealth of information available since 1717, when the Grand Lodge of England was opened. In those days Masons were secretive and used the pigpen cipher ("pigpen" because it required pigpen-like grids to draw the, in order to substitute letters). Confederates in the American Civil War also used it.

The Set Square and Compass is the main symbol of Freemasonry. The compass is a symbol of virtue and the

square is used for trying accuracy. The central letter G is for God or for "geometry." The triangle is an important symbol, especially if there is an all-seeing eye inside it. It is a symbol of the all-knowing God, and of spiritual insight and higher knowledge.

American Masons possess "three immovable jewels," which are the Square, the Level, and the Plumb Line. These represent spiritual rather than physical building.

ELIPHAS LÉVI

The man who was to create a basis for all things occult was Eliphas Lévi (1810–75). Lévi's original name was Alphonse Louis Constant. He studied for the priesthood, but was unsuited and gave up. In England he met Bulwer Lytton, fantasy novelist and contender for the prize of worst ever writer in English. Lévi was a great popularizer, and from his day there developed a cult

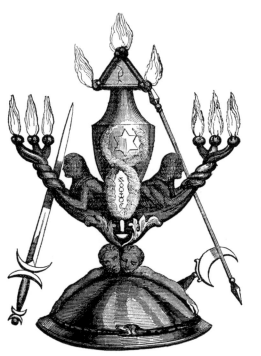

of personality in the esoteric and occult.

Lévi's drawings and writings created a basis for Madame Blavatsky, Aleister Crowley and others. Lévi's works included *Transcendental Magic: Its Doctrine and Rituals.* This was wide-ranging — covering magic from the Vedas, Egypt, Assyria, and world history.

A new interpretation of Cabala came from Eliphas Lévi and the Hermetic Order of the Golden Dawn. Cabala was mixed with other esoteric ideas to create the Hermetic Cabala with the Sephiroth as aspects of an astral, magical world of initiation.

Lévi believed in "astral light" — control of which would enable control of all things. He wanted to apply it to people — in the same way that a mesmerist can get an individual who is hypnotized to believe that plain water has various flavors.

ABOVE: Lévi's illustration of magical instruments.

RIGHT: Lévi's Göetic circle of black invocations is eccentric and confusing, using a mixture of invented material, Christian and black magic symbols.

OPPOSITE LEFT: The Set Square and Compass, the main symbol of Freemasonry.

OPPOSITE RIGHT: Eliphas Lévi, born Alphonse Louis Constant, was a French occult author and magician.

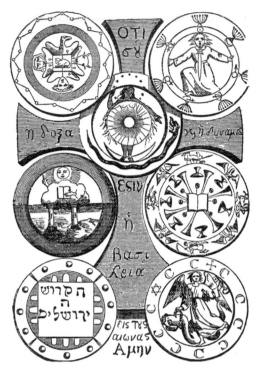

star; an ouroboros (the snake with its tail in its mouth symbolizes regeneration and immortality, infinity, and unity) that stretches around the base of the lamp; and the seven sigils for the planets are found between a pair of sphinxes.

The source of the signatures of the demons he reproduced is a document used at the trial of Urban Grandier. Grandier was a priest, burned as a witch in 1634. He was accused of signing a pact with the devil; the pact produced as evidence was written in Latin (backwards!) and clearly signed by

LEFT: Lévi's illustration of magical symbols.

BELOW LEFT: Macrocosm and microcosm entwined in the Seal of Solomon, surrounded by the Ouroboros serpent. From Eliphas Lévi, Transcendental Magic, *1896.*

OPPOSITE LEFT: Lévi's creation, Baphomet (the Sabbatic goat).

OPPOSITE RIGHT: The modern symbol of the Theosophical Society.

Lévi's painstaking illustrations show the blazing five-pointed star and the Seal of Solomon. He believed that they had the power to chain rebellious spirits. Lévi's pentagram contains symbols of the Gnosis, figures of occultism, and cabalistic keys of prophecy.

He illustrated the instruments required for ceremonial magic — a lamp, sword, dagger, and wand. The wand should never be mentioned, and should be treated with great circumspection. The lamp bears several symbols: there is a six-pointed

Grandier, the devil, and assorted demons. The signatures are complicated, as are all sigils for demons. Of course, a more rational explanation of the document could be that Grandier, a curate in Loudun, incurred the displeasure of Cardinal Richelieu by writing a satire and by his political support of greater independence for Loudun. At this point, a convent of nuns nearby began to complain of diabolical possession, accusing the priest Grandier, who was tried and executed.

Lévi thought that all signs of evil augury are in the northern region of the sky — a serpent or dragon and two bears. He said these are true hieroglyphs of tyranny, pillage, and oppression, and account for why Rome suffered from the depredations of so many enemies. If he was correct, many other aspects of ill-starred European disasters could be accounted for.

The word "disaster" derives from *dis* and *astro*, *dis* meaning "away, without," and *astro* meaning "star" (Latin *astrum* and Greek *astron*). Thus, a disaster is a calamity stemming from unfavorable planetary positions. The stars also influenced health; influenza for example is the Italian for "influence."

Lévi's creation, Baphomet (the Sabbatic goat), is viewed by many as a major symbol of black magic. Lévi, who created it, does not appear to have had evil in mind. He said it is a symbolic representation of the absolute. The goat's head has a pentagram on its forehead, with a symbol of light in the one point at the top. The hands form a sign for hermeticism, pointing to a white and a black moon, symbolizing mercy with justice. One arm is male and the other female, as both attributes are united in the same symbol. Lévi said that they are like the arms of "the androgyn of Khunrath." The upper arm is marked "solve," meaning save, set free; the lower arm reads "coagula" — meaning to impede.

Lévi said the head "expresses the horror of the sinner whose materially acting, solely responsible part has to bear the punishment exclusively; because the soul is insensitive according to its nature and can only suffer when it materializes."

The rod symbolizes eternal life. Lévi called this the Baphomet of Mendes. "Baphomet" is claimed by some to be a mispronunciation of Mohammed. Mendes is a Greek name for Djedet, an Egyptian god who was actually a ram deity. The symbol was entirely personal to Lévi, and his account of the symbolism of his creation makes it difficult to see it as an evil, black magic sign.

MADAME BLAVATSKY AND THEOSOPHY
Lévi's works influenced Madame Blavatsky (1831–91), who claimed to have made extraordinary travels during which she learned eastern occult traditions. She arrived in New York in 1873 when spiritualism was fashionable, and displayed psychic abilities — including mediumship, levitation, clairvoyance, and materialization. In

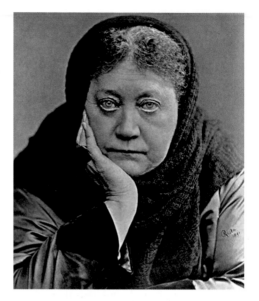

1875 she founded the Theosophical Society with Colonel Olcott. The Society's beliefs melded religious ideas to Tantric Buddhism and Brahmanism. The importance of symbols can be seen in the emblem of the Society.

Within the circle of the ouroboros are interlinked triangles, a lighter-colored one pointing up and a darker one down. These symbolize the descent of spirit into matter and its re-emergence from this confinement — the inseparable nature of spirit and matter, or the struggle between light and dark forces. The placing of the triangles within the circle symbolizes the universe and the manifestation of the deity in time and space. The three lines and three angles of each triangle show the triple aspects of spirit, existence, consciousness, and bliss; and the three aspects of matter — mobility, resistance, and rhythm. The whole can also be seen as a six-pointed star, a sign of creation and spiritual and physical consciousness.

The Ankh is an Egyptian hieroglyph for "life." Here it is regarded as a Tau, a T-shaped cross symbolizing matter, with a circle that symbolizes spirit and life. Together they make a cross, the spirit crucified and raised triumphant.

The "Om" is the Hindu symbol of the Absolute, the primal syllable, the creative word. It recalls the Gospel according to St John: "In the beginning was the Word, and the Word was with God, and the Word was God."

Taken as a whole, the emblem looks toward inner perception, and speaks to the heart and intuition of each individual, calling forth the divine. It is a synthesis of great cosmic principles to bring us to realize our divine nature.

After the death of Madame Blavatsky the Society split into two and subsequently many splinter groups have formed.

ANTHROPOSOPHY

During the late nineteenth century esotericism was exported all over the world. Madame Blavatsky had settled in India, but maintained contact with Europe and America. In Germany and Austria, Theosophical circles met and welcomed cognoscenti from America and elsewhere. Rudolf Steiner, who led the Theosophists in Austria and Germany, was interested in methods of

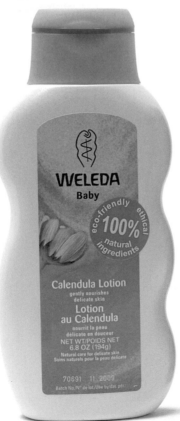

RIGHT: Aleister Crowley

BELOW RIGHT: One of the symbols used by the order of the Golden Dawn.

OPPOSITE LEFT: Madame Blavatsky.

OPPOSITE RIGHT: The Weleda logo designed by Rudolf Steiner.

developing spiritual life within the individual.

The parting of the ways came because Steiner was Christian and European and unable to accept the neo-Hindu notions of Annie Besant, who was at that time leading the Theosophists in India. Her pronouncements on her protégé Krishnamurti as a new messiah were unacceptable to Steiner, who left the organization and founded Anthroposophy. He was fascinated by symbolism, and published four lectures on occult signs and symbols. Steiner had a massive range of interests, including spirituality, education, and medicine, and he was the designer of the logo now used for the Weleda range of homeopathic and health products.

HERMETIC ORDER OF THE GOLDEN DAWN
Lévi was a major influence in the beliefs of the Hermetic Order of the Golden Dawn, founded in 1888. Members believed it was possible to control the forces of nature with magic. The Irish poet W. B. Yates and Aleister Crowley were members. Israel Regardie, one-time secretary to Crowley, published books on the ideas of the order, a mixture of Cabala, ritual magic, and spiritual ideas derived from alchemy.

Modern Golden Dawn organizations and individual practitioners still exist: one organization has its logo patented at the U.S. Patent and Trademark Office, and far from being secretive, access to its symbols and philosophies is available on the Internet and as specialist software.

ALEISTER CROWLEY
Aleister Crowley (1857–1947) has been called "the wickedest man in the world" — although this seems a little overblown even for a contemporary of Hitler (1889–1945) and Stalin (1878–1953). Crowley liked to believe he was a reincarnation of Lévi (there were only six months between Lévi's death and Crowley's birth).

Crowley joined the Hermetic Order of the Golden Dawn, but had a dispute

ALCHEMY, MAGIC & RITUALS

In 1920 Crowley founded the Abbey of Thelema in Sicily. Inspiration came from Francois Rabelais' novel *Gargantua and Pantagruel*, which contains a fictitious philosophy of "Do what thou wilt." Philosophy, the occult, mysticism, Cabala, Hermeticism, and angels were all crucial in forming the law of the organization. The discovery and manifestation of the true will of every individual was central. Members were given details of their duties. An important symbol of Thelema was a

with a rival, both men creating talismans and amulets with the Seal of Solomon, and both claiming to have called forth armies of demons and angels.

To Crowley, "Magick is the science and art of causing change to occur in conformity with the will." It was spelled with a "k" to distinguish it from stage magic.

Crowley studied Enochian magic using the journals of John Dee, and produced a highly symbolic and hard-to-understand work on the subject. Dee had taken down everything said by his collaborator Edward Kelley during scrying sessions. During these sessions, it was claimed, they took dictation from angels. Squared tablets were drawn with runes in each square; these were maps of the invisible spheres surrounding our world. The magic stemming from this source was called Enochian, as the Biblical Enoch talked with angels.

unicursal hexagram, a six-point star, drawn without removing the pen from the paper, rather than drawn as two interlocking triangles. The ability to draw the symbol in one continuous movement (as with the pentagram) was considered significant in ritual magic. Crowley added a rose with five petals at the center, symbolizing a pentacle and the divine feminine.

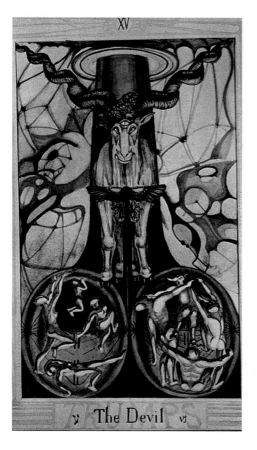

The six points of the star and five petals total eleven, a number of divine union, a personal sigil of Crowley and the number for magic.

Crowley also founded the Ordo Templis Orientis, an early 20th-century society intended as a Freemason offshoot, but organized by Crowley on the lines of his Thelema: "Do what thou want shall be the whole of the law. Love is the law, love under will." His rational basis for universal brotherhood and religion reveals "all that is known about the universe by means of a simple yet sublime symbolism, artistically arranged." Instruction is "by allegory and symbol in the profound mysteries of nature" to enable people to find their true identity.

Crowley used symbols from all over the world, from history, religion, science, and philosophy. The Thoth Tarot, which Crowley and Lady Frieda Harris produced between 1938 and 1943, uses surreal imagery.

In the years since his death, a myriad of organizations concerned with magic, Wicca, Cabala, and new age philosophies have been created. Magic today is both popular and

highly profitable: in fact, it is all so accessible that perhaps it should be called exoteric. For more than forty years it has been possible to study Christian and western esotericism at universities in England, France, and Holland, so it is hardly secretive.

Magic happens every day; remember Arthur C. Clark's third law: "Any sufficiently advanced technology is indistinguishable from magic."

THE NAZIS
Nazis had radically different sources for inventing tradition. Sadly, some esoteric ideas became enmeshed in Ariosophy, which was the notion of the ethnic wisdom of the Aryans.

LEFT: The Devil tarot card from the Thoth deck designed by Crowley and illustrated by Lady Frieda Harris.

OPPOSITE: Hitler and the Brownshirts, Braunschweig, Germany, 1931.

The Nazis are said to have been opposed to the occult, though many associate them with the black arts. Nazis thought the esoteric organizations had the *wrong* invented traditions, so members of assorted churches — Jehovah's Witnesses, Jews, Freemasons, Rosicrucians, Theosophists, Anthroposophists, astrologers, and occultists — were moved to the camps in large numbers. The druids were closed down. They didn't serve the ethnic mythology of Nazi Germany.

The Nazis invented their own traditions, using Nordic and Teutonic myths, ideas about the purity of the Nordic race, or Aryans, eugenics, racial regeneration, blood and soil, *lebensraum* (land the Nazis felt they needed to acquire), and reconquering lost lands.

The Aryan race, which Madame Blavatsky had considered one of the "Root Races" from Atlantis, was elevated as a model of racial purity. Nazis sought contact with subterranean super-beings. Nietzsche's *übermensch* (often translated as "superman," or "over-man," though neither is exactly right) was also part of the picture.

The Thule Society was an

organization devoted to seeking super-beings, and for a time was in contact with the Theosophists. They developed a particular taste for racial theories and hatred of the Jews. They used the symbol of the *hakenkreuz* — a swastika with a dagger superimposed on it.

Hitler was eager to acquire powerful symbols such as the Spear of Longinus, reputed to be the spear used to pierce Christ's side at the crucifixion. This relic (ancient, but not that ancient) had been in the hands of various rulers for centuries and of course, it is said that to hold the spear is to hold power. Frustrated by his early poverty, and his inability to be able to study art in the city, Hitler hated Vienna and seized the spear as soon as he entered the city following the *anschluss*. He moved the spear to Nuremberg. As the war ended the Americans confiscated it, and it is said that Hitler committed suicide within the half-hour.

LEFT: Hitler at a rally in Dortmund, Germany in 1933.

OPPOSITE: Swastikas are used in an Indian Rangoli on a doorstep in London, England to celebrate the New Year.

Some believe the Nazis would have liked the grail too — but Indiana Jones is not necessarily a historically accurate source. However, it is true that Nazis sent archaeologists on digs, seeking proof of the glorious Aryan origins. Senior Nazis were irritated that they could not annex Greece and Rome as antecedents, finding only dreary broken pots associated with Aryans. Expeditions were launched to Tibet and the Arctic and Antarctic, seeking evidence of the Aryans and of a city called Shambhala. Shambhala is a Tibetan Buddhist idea. His Holiness the Dalai Lama says that it is arrived at by spiritual means, and is not a place in geographical terms.

The Nazis were interested in runes. "Armanen" runes were "seen" in 1902 with his inner eye by Guido von List, his sight having been impaired by an

The swastika emblem was used in Neolithic times, and has been found in excavations at Troy, dating from 1000 BCE. It is found in China, India, England, Germany, and Greece, and was used by Native Americans. It was positive, symbolizing the sun, good fortune, success, joy, power and strength, life itself. It shows the eternal nature of God, pointing in all directions and showing his omnipresence.

It is still valued and used by Hindus and Buddhists. Indian businessmen inscribe it on new account books as they begin a new year, and wedding invitations are decorated with it. Indian housewives use it in their designs for the Festival of Light.

In the First World War it was used by the American 45th Division on shoulder patches.

Because of its use by the Nazis, the swastika is now taboo in some countries. The swastika became a symbol of the Nazi Party in Germany in 1920 and thus acquired new symbolic values — violence, death, hate, and anti-Semitism.

Hitler designed his own emblem, a swastika on a white circle with a red background. He used it on his personal banner, to compete with the communist hammer and sickle.

operation. No scholars give credence to this set of runes, but it was to have importance. Its symbols were used by the Nazis to great effect. The SS rune signs were Armanen runes. Other symbols were the eagle on top of a swastika; the black SS uniform; the *totenkopf* (death's head, or skull and crossbones, worn on rings); and the Iron Cross. A symbol rarely seen is the Black Sun, an image made up of multiple swastikas, found on a floor at Wewelsburg, the SS cult center. These symbols horrify most people, though groups of people with neo-Nazi ideas continue to use and develop them.

The Nazis had another set of symbols — for those who were not part of Nazism. Nazi symbols were imposed on them too: the ghastly system of yellow stars, pink triangles, and other classificatory symbols worn in the camps. A whole system was prepared to classify those they saw as inferior, subhuman *untermensch*.

WITCHCRAFT

Witchcraft is the source of many heated
and emotive debates. Alan Macfarlane,
Professor of Anthropological Science
at the University of Cambridge,
observes, "Most human societies believe
in witchcraft." It is "intellectually and
socially attractive." When bad things
happen you can identify who was
responsible and punish or kill them —
though it is clear that the professor
believes that scientific method is the
path to knowledge and can recognize
illusion. His work *Witchcraft in Tudor
and Stewart England* (1970) shows
how social and economic conditions
gave rise to beliefs about witches and
their subsequent persecution. Witch
trials spread the belief that witches
can fly, and that they have "familiars,"
often cats.

Casting spells is an ancient idea:
Hammurabi's law code specified the
punishment for casting a spell in
2000 BCE. The Bible mentions sorcerers

*RIGHT: Witches ride through the murky air,
from William Harrison Ainsworth's*
Lancashire Witches.

*OPPPOSITE: An inscrutable black cat —
not really witching, just pretending.*

and a necromancer, the Witch of Endor. It also commands "Thou shalt not suffer a witch to live." Some believe that Shakespeare's witches in *Macbeth* chant effective spells.

German witches come out on Walpurgisnacht (April 30th – May 1st) and convene to celebrate. From Germany comes the word "hex," from *hexen*, to use witchcraft. Scandinavian, German and Austrian, and Pennsylvania Dutch designs often include symbols to protect against the evil eye, protect home and hearth, and cure ailments.

The symbols favored by witches are the Star of David, planets, hearts, and tulips. Hearts represent love, and tulips faith or fertility. Symbolic birds called *distelfinks* are also popular. Colors are symbolic: blue for protection, green for abundance, red for emotion, and white for purity.

Witchcraft is found in every society. African practitioners who produce "cures" are crudely called witch doctors, and patients believe that evil witches cause AIDS and cancer. Is the witch a benevolent healer or a wicked old woman?

Modern witchcraft, or Wicca in the English-speaking world, owes much to writings dating from 1954 by Gerald Gardner (a retired British civil servant). Gardner claimed that that witchcraft was a survival from pre-Christian paganism, but this has never

RIGHT: Herbs and flowers used for spells and potions: rosebuds, passionflower, lemon balm, white lilies, and lavender.

OPPOSITE: Latvian midsummer celebrations — garlanded with oak leaves.

been proved.

Another ancestor of modern witchcraft was Margaret Murray, a respected scholar at UCL whose book *The Witch Cult in Western Europe* was first published in 1921. There was severe academic criticism of her interpretation and of the way she manipulated evidence. Murray sought proof of a goddess, but during the entire period when witch trials were conducted, there was never mention of one. She twisted evidence to portray the horned god as the Satan of the witch trials.

Outside academic circles her book was a bestseller and believed by many. Her authenticity was enhanced by her contribution to the *Encyclopaedia Britannica*, regarded as an unimpeachable source.

Further ancestors of the cult were

the novelists Dion Fortune, Robert Graves, H.P. Lovecraft, and Denis Wheatley. Aleister Crowley and the fashionable esoteric organizations of the day were also influential in the development of the cult.

The beginnings of the cult were in 1920s Britain, but it really became popular after the 1950s. Many were interested in matters "spiritual" as opposed to traditional religion. In 1951 the Witchcraft Act of 1735 was repealed, mainly because it prohibited mediumship, thus it was inconvenient for Spiritualists.

Gardner and Murray placed importance upon covens. Murray insisted that these had thirteen members, though she tweaked the evidence to prove it.

The word "coven" had no previous association with witches: it meant a

ABOVE: A besom — a broom for sweeping or flying?

LEFT: The pentacle is a popular symbol associated with magic and witchcraft.

OPPOSITE: Triple moon and goddess on a cauldron.

meeting. Most devotees of modern Wicca are not members of covens and follow their own paths, so symbols, beliefs, and practices vary.

Murray outlined four major festivals, though nowadays there are eight. These are four festivals from the Gaelic or Celtic calendar and four from the solar calendar. They are celebrated with appropriate symbols of the season. Spring flowers are for Imbolc and the spring equinox; Maypoles, Green Men, and crowns of flowers for Beltane; oak leaves for the return of the god at the summer equinox.

Sickles, wheat, bread, and corn dollies are for Lammastide, and discarded antlers, fallen leaves, and pine cones for the autumn equinox; Samhain is black and brown with blackened mirrors, twigs, crystal balls, and cauldrons: a festival of the dead. The mid-winter solstice is Yule, a risky time when death is common as the elderly and animals succumb to the cold: the Yule log burns for twelve days. It's good to eat, drink, and make merry — after all, there's much to celebrate and summer will come again.

Modern witches select their own, personal symbols. The awen is popular. It is drawn as three rays of light,

converging at the top. The awen symbolizes harmony, eagerness to learn, and inspiration. The most popular symbol is the pentagram, or pentacle, a five-point star enclosed in a circle, representing the four elements, earth, air, fire, and water and spirit at the pinnacle of the star. A magic circle has the four cardinal elements at the four directions.

Other symbols are the tools of the craft. The besom (broom) is for purification (though the young will see besoms as essential gear for quidditch). Brooms are also for marriage rites, a custom also found in African American history.

The cauldron speaks of plenty, the earth mother, transformation, and the womb of the goddess.

The wand is a symbol of air. Various knives are used: a black-handled knife called an *athame* (a Gardner coinage) and a *boline*.

The *boline* is a sickle-shaped knife associated with druids — like the one used by Getafix in the Asterix books to collect mistletoe. Devotees keep a "Book of Shadows." Such a book was described by Gardner as "a personal cookbook of spells" that have worked for the owner.

The god and goddess are symbolized by the sun and moon and may be manifested in the body of a priest or priestess through divine possession — this is the meaning of "Drawing down the Moon."

Eyes

The eye is a very powerful symbol: there are cultures that tolerate no depiction of eyes and deface them when they are depicted. It is an ancient symbol. The Egyptian god Horus offers protection with his eye symbol. It was placed on mummification incisions to "heal" them.

LEFT: A modern Athane or witch's knife.

OPPOSITE: The eye of Horus.

Symbolic eyes are used for good and evil. In India, God grants his grace with a glance, and devotees gain merit from a *darshan* — seeing a deity. Buddha and holy men are shown with a third eye — the gentle eye of spiritual wisdom. The Hindu Lord Siva once saved the world, and can reduce wrongdoers to a heap of ashes with his third eye.

The act of eye bestowing — placing the eyes on a Hindu deity —requires a special ceremony. It completes the *murti* (image) and establishes power.

The evil eye is feared, but is not necessarily malevolent and spiteful. Asian belief is that gazing too long and adoringly on someone or something can induce love in it.

There are a huge collection of amulets and symbolic objects to avert

the evil eye. Spitting, wearing red, or carrying salt or coal in your pocket are recommended. *Kajaal*, eye black, is useful too.

The Hamsa/Hamesh hand is a Jewish/Muslim amulet. It can be reinforced in power by having a double ceramic eye on the palm. For added security, some people wear bracelets of eyes (two or three at a time sometimes). There is also a lovely blue amulet found in Istanbul, to hang in the home. If it ever gets cracked, it has done its job and you need a new one. Ceramic or glass eyes say "I can see what you are doing." And they deflect the curse back to the sender.

Amulets can be reinforced in power by having a double ceramic eye on the palm, or, for added security, some people wear bracelets of eyes, again, two or three at a time.

The digits of the Islamic amulet recall the five pillars of Islam. Some say the thumb represents the Prophet and the fingers represent his family:

LEFT: Hand of Fatima Islamic silver pendant.

OPPOSITE: Eye beads to protect against the evil eye.

SUPERNATURAL SIGNS, SYMBOLS, AND CODES

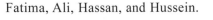

LEFT: Eyes on the prows of boats in Kerala, India. One has a baby Siva.

BELOW: A traditional eye painted on a boat in Cyprus.

The Aztec had a death eye symbol, a circle with a line across it. Death was not to be feared, and to die in battle or in ritual was considered good.

The eye symbol is used by business: CBS, AOL, and the television series *Big Brother* all have symbols that feature an eye.

GRAVES AND DEATH

Death is symbolized in the west by the Grim Reaper, a skeleton with a hood

Fatima, Ali, Hassan, and Hussein.

Porcelain eyes are popular in Latin America. In the southwestern United States and Mexico, Huichol people have a special amulet, the *Ojo de Dios*, to protect people and homes.

Boats often have eyes painted on the prow. The eye is to find the route across the ocean, to find fish, and to protect the crew from danger, misfortune, and ill luck. Eyes were painted on ancient Egyptian boats. Dragon boats have their eyes opened for racing and then closed to allow them to rest.

and scythe, and by skeletons, corpses, coffins, and skulls. "Alas, poor Yorick! I knew him, Horatio," says Hamlet, lifting the skull.

Father Time is relentless. The old man and his scythe are symbols of death, gathering in those whose time has come. Sometimes he has an hourglass, to emphasize man's fleeting lifespan. The scythe originated with Chronos, the Greek god, hence *chrono-*, pertaining to time.

Nations have memorials and military graveyards for fallen soldiers. A Cenotaph, meaning "empty tomb," symbolizes many lost men. The tomb of the unknown warrior marks the grave of just one, in Kipling's phrase "Known only unto God."

In Asia, Yama is the Lord of Death, symbolizing the inevitability of death and the impermanence of attachment in life. In some cultures, Yama holds a wheel of life, with six sections symbolizing the realms of existence, the gods, demi-gods,

humans, animals, ghosts, and hell. Twelve outer sections symbolize causality: these include the sensory organs and human foibles such as desire, craving, and ignorance

Objects that mark the passage of time, sundials, clocks, and hourglasses, also tell us that life is fleeting. *Memento mori* — "remember you must die" — is a

ABOVE: The Arlington National Cemetery, resting place of American heroes.

LEFT: The Grim Reaper on an astronomical clock, Campanile Duomo, Messina, Sicily.

LEFT: 18th-century embroidered tangka of the dharmapala Yama.

BELOW: Skulls and crosses — Memento mori.

OPPOSITE: Sir John de Montacute died in 1389. Having fought at Crecy in 1346 and Poitiers in 1356 he merits a lion supporting his feet.

theme in art, often with beauty shown alongside death.

Graves are usually marked. Ancient English churches have effigies

on tombs, showing the occupant. Effigies and brasses, which are flat metal engravings set into the floor, give information about armor, costume, and heraldry, although as they were not necessarily created at the time of the death, they may be inaccurate. If the effigy has a dog supporting his feet, it is a sign he died naturally, but a lion signifies that he died in battle.

Graveyards offer contrasting insights in their choice of statues and symbols. An ornate nineteenth-century gravestone probably bankrupted the family, but it shows how respectable they were. Père Lachaise in Paris is believed to be the world's most visited cemetery. Oscar Wilde lies there, beneath a strange winged messenger sculpted by Epstein. The entire edifice is covered with lipstick kisses, which presumably symbolize the feelings of the kissers. The nearby grave of Victor Noir is a fertility symbol of sorts, and until it was fenced off his prostrate figure was a magnet for infertile women.

DAY OF THE DEAD

The Day of the Dead is celebrated in Central and South America, and its origins lie in the pre-Columbian era. It sounds gloomy, but is full of life, happiness, food and drink, flowers, and family. Marigolds are especially associated with the festival as they attract souls and draw them back.

Special "bread of the dead" is made in the shape of the skull and crossbones. Numerous chocolate and sugar skeletons and skulls are presented to the dead and the living. Symbolic pottery, puppets, skulls and skeletons, and candles are sold. Offerings including food and drink, portraits, personal items, clothing, and favorite foods. Toys are brought for children. There are visits to graves, which are decorated, and picnics are held at the site, where the family recall incidents, often comical, associated

LEFT: A Day of the Dead altar in a traditional Mexican home.

OPPOSITE: An Aztec Indian in traditional dress performing a spiritual ceremony using smoke on the Day of the Dead in Mexico City.

OPPOSITE: A classic Mexican figure in a Day of the Dead parade in a Zapotec village.

RIGHT: In kolams *the mathematical and geometric shapes and symbols are drawn with one continuous line.*

with the dead person, who it is believed can hear and appreciate what they say.

KOLAMS, *RANGOLIS,* AND OTHERS
In India, *kolams* and *rangolis* are paintings, usually done on the floor. South Indian women, especially Brahmins, used to have a purifying bath first thing in the morning, and then clean outside the house before decorating the ground outside the door, where others might have a doormat, with a *kolam* painting. Nowadays, many women no longer have the time and possibly the inclination to follow this tradition. *Kolams* are harder to find than they used to be, though some modern housewives use vinyl ones, which somewhat negate the whole tradition of having a symbol showing that life was fleeting, for traditionally each day's *kolam* was washed away and replaced next morning. However, *kolams* are drawn for festive and

SUPERNATURAL SIGNS, SYMBOLS, AND CODES

ceremonial occasions, but never in periods of mourning. There is a complex symbolism as lines represent creation, sustenance, and destruction, mystic powers, and astrological influences. They deliver lessons on good and evil.

Traditional *rangolis* were quite small, about two square feet (.1858 sq. m). Nowadays they can cover large areas of streets or spaces in the big hotels. *Rangolis* are associated with the festival of *Diwali*, and are painted in the hope of attracting Lakshmi, goddess of wealth. A few years ago the painting medium was

mostly foodstuffs, rice flour, pulses, and spices. The white rice powder symbolized purity. The artist works by laying out the pattern in dots and then joining the points to make an unbroken line. These days, garish powder paints and glitter add texture and pizzazz. *Rangolis* symbolized impermanence, for they were rapidly destroyed, and *maya* illusion. They attract deities and warn away evil spirits.

The designs used in *kolams* and *rangolis* vary in different parts of the sub-continent, but they often involve geometric shapes such as triangles

LEFT: A woman in India creating a Rangoli.

OPPOSITE LEFT: Buddhist monks make complex mandalas — patterns in sand.

OPPOSITE RIGHT: Australian Aboriginal painting on bark. Near a palm tree in the jungle, two female Mimi spirits hunt for bush food at Gudgerama.

pointing upward symbolizing masculinity and downward symbolizing feminity. Fish symbolize wealth, and lotus blossoms are associated with Lakshmi and purity. Circles, swastikas, footprints, trees, flowers, animals, and birds are also common motifs.

Very similar to *kolams* are voodoo *vévé,* which are intricate symbols of *loa* (deities). Each *loa* has its own symbol, which is traced out in crushed eggshells, flour, cornmeal, or even gunpowder. The designs and material vary for different ceremonies. Like *kolams, vévé* are impermanent and are erased by the feet of people dancing in the ceremony.

Sand painting is a feature of Navaho culture. Before beginning the work, the practitioner must be purified. Colored sands are then used to create an image of Father Sky and Mother

sources of food and water. In modern times, the paintings are more likely to be permanent and for sale.

Earth, deeply important symbols showing that everything is conceived in the sky and comes to pass on earth. They are used as aids to healing, and patients may be placed upon the picture or rubbed with sand from it. As in India, the design is rapidly obliterated.

Sand paintings are found in Tibetan Buddhism, and monks produce complex *mandalas*, geometric sand designs symbolic of the universe, using special instruments. The *mandalas* are extremely complex and the rules for carrying out the work are strict. They symbolize Buddhist cosmology and objects of reverence.

In Mexico, sand paintings are produced as part of the rituals of the Day of the Dead. Very colorful skeletons are popular.

Australian Aboriginal people have "dot paintings," which are similar to sand paintings. They are created using sand, seeds, flowers, feathers, and other items that came to hand. While the creative process is in progress, the elders sing explanations, thus educating their young. The various symbols are explained, and creation myths, history, and clan heritage revealed. They also convey practical knowledge concerning

CHAPTER THREE
HERALDRY, GUILDS, LIVERY & COMPANIES

The Bayeux Tapestry is crowded with knights, but the confusion of battle stems from their lack of shield devices to aid recognition. Duke William has to remove his helmet to be distinguishable in the melée. This was dangerous, so his successors developed heraldry, and to this day the language of heraldry is Norman French. It is used to describe a coat of arms — the shields, crests, supporters, mottoes, and other features. Heraldry flourished in Medieval and Renaissance Europe, a period when symbolism was hugely important. The "sympathies" of heraldic colors were the same as those held by alchemists, so the colors, called tinctures, related to planets, gemstones, signs of the zodiac, and so on. Blue, *azure*, linked to Jupiter, sapphire and to the element air, while *gules* (red) linked to Mars, ruby, and fire. Two metals, gold and silver, were used alongside the tinctures.

STANDARDS

From ancient times, armies carried standards for recognition. In Britain, "colors" are carried by the infantry — hence the summer ceremony "Trooping the Colour" in London, where the color is paraded before the soldiers to ensure that they recognize it. The cavalry regiments have standards and guidons (from the French *guide*

HERALDRY, GUILDS, LIVERY & COMPANIES

OPPOSITE: Trooping the Colour.

BELOW: An elephant battling a serpent from a 14th-century book of Bestiaries.

RIGHT: A very fierce dragon took on all comers.

homme). Battle honors were added to the flags, which then became a part of regimental history. The flags were consecrated and could be used as altars in the field. They are never destroyed, and old ones were placed in chapels or cathedrals. It is a disgrace to lose the colors, so they are carefully guarded.

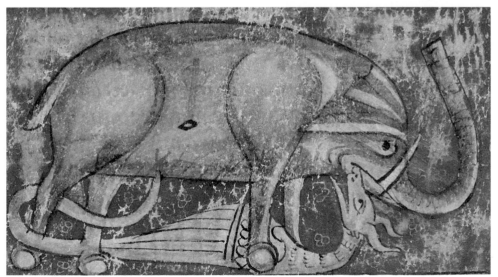

HERALDIC ANIMALS

Medieval Bestiaries (books of beasts) contain well-known animals and also some fabulous, mythical creatures. Bestiaries usually included a picture of the beast, some natural history, and a moral lesson. It was believed that every living thing had a meaning so, like the language of flowers, there was a language of animals, and from these qualities, suitable heraldic mascots were found. When a coat of arms was granted, the symbols were chosen to

match the qualities of the recipient, or to symbolize what it was hoped he might become. In some cases, they also displayed a sense of humor.

HERALDIC BEASTS

A martlet is a footless bird, needing no feet as it is permanently in flight and will not rest until victory is won. It was bestowed by Edward III on knights who were unceasing in their efforts and were victorious in battle in France.

The martlet is a symbol used for a fourth son. The eldest son inherited, the second and third went into the army and the church, and the fourth was left to make his own living. Marks exist for up to ten sons. A diamond is a symbol for a woman.

A dragon has the head of a serpent, a forked tongue, and the body of a lion, with scales and talons on the feet. It symbolizes a defender who is brave and protective. In Medieval Europe, it was seen as a symbol of forthcoming disaster and associated with anger and envy. In the East, it was seen as a harbinger of good luck and fortune. The Mesoamerican feathered serpent deity, Quetzalcoatl, is seen as the one who gave knowledge to mankind, and as a symbol of death and rebirth.

Unicorns, symbols of purity and innocence, are often used as heraldic bearers. Their popularity is also vouched for by the tapestries at the Musée de Cluny in Paris. These show a lady with a unicorn on her left and a lion on the right. A monkey often appears too, along with many other animals. The pictures are variously interpreted, but are thought to symbolize the six senses: hearing, sight, taste, touch, smell, and love. The tapestries have a mille-fleur background, literally meaning a "thousand flowers"; with such a wealth of symbols one is left feeling inadequate, not recognizing what would have been perfectly clear to those who made and first saw the tapestries.

The wyvern is a two-legged winged creature, somewhat like a dragon. It symbolizes strength, valor, and protection. The griffin has the body of

LEFT: The Lady with the Unicorn, Musée de Cluny, Paris.

RIGHT: City of London griffins.

Florence's symbol is a red *fleur de lys*. In modern times, it is a symbol of the Scouting Movement, and appears on many flags and logos.

HERALDRY TODAY

Heraldry in Britain has been presided over by the College of Arms since 1484, but antiquity does not preclude modern interpretations.

Sir Paul McCartney's arms include symbols of Liverpool and his music: a "Liver bird" holds a guitar in its claw. No one is sure as to the species of the Liverpudlian symbol, the Liver (rhymes with driver) bird. It appeared on a seal in the 1350s and has been thought to be a cormorant, or eagle, or a mythical bird.

The four Beatles are remembered in four curved emblems resembling

a lion, but the wings, head, and talons of an eagle. It is swift, intelligent, valiant, and brave.

THE POSITIONS OF ANIMALS

In heraldry, animals are shown in various positions. Lions or horses can be *rampant*: standing on hind legs, looking forwards. *Passant* animals stand on three legs with one leg raised, looking forward to symbolize resolution or determination. *Salient* refers to a leaping animal, perhaps pouncing, symbolizing valor and willingness to fight bravely.

FLOWERS AND TREES

Flowers and trees may be used in heraldry. The *fleur de lys*, a stylized lily or iris flower, was usually associated with France and French royalty, but is now international in use. The city of

LEFT: A red lion rampant on the royal flag of Scotland.

OPPOSITE LEFT: Beautiful fleur de lys *from the* Book of Hours, *c.1500, from the Wake Collection.*

OPPOSITE RIGHT: Dizzying numbers of fleurs de lys *decorate the Abbaye St. Michel de Frigolet, Provence, France.*

beetles' backs. The motto is *Ecce Cor Meum* "behold my heart." Sir Elton John's arms include a keyboard and a soccer ball.

Americans sometimes use the word "crest" instead of coat of arms. In England "crest" is just one part, usually placed on top of a helmet, ensuring that the wearer was recognizable and avoiding Duke William's problems. The main part is called the escutcheon or shield.

In North America, the Society for Creative Anachronism, a reenactment group, have a simple crest — "Or, a laurel wreath vert."

GUILDS AND LIVERY COMPANIES

Guilds were associations of craftsmen found in ancient India, Egypt, Rome, China, and the Muslim world. Between

OPPOSITE: The Lord Mayor used to ride a horse, but in 1757 he was unseated by a flower girl and has ridden in a gilded coach ever since.

BELOW: The Vintners' and Dyers' companies boatmen on the River Thames, England.

about 1100 and the 1900s guilds were active in Europe, and some vestiges of

their privileges remain to this day.

In Medieval England, "livery" was food, drink, and clothing provided to officers of great houses. The word came to mean distinctive clothing and badges symbolizing privileges and protection, so bodies governing different trades became known as livery companies. Companies provide companionship, education and oversee standards within the profession. In 1878 a meeting of livery companies established the "City and Guilds" examinations for technical education. Changes in trade and industry have caused something of a decline: apprentices learning traditional skills are less common, but City and Guilds have modernized to fit the needs of the times.

The Worshipful Company of Goldsmiths in London still assay precious metals and hallmark them with symbols, and the Worshipful Company of Fishmongers keep an eye on hygiene at London's major fish market.

One hundred and eighteen Livery Companies exist in the City of London. Companies participate in the Lord Mayor's Show, when the Mayor's gilded coach is taken out of the Museum of London and drawn through the streets,

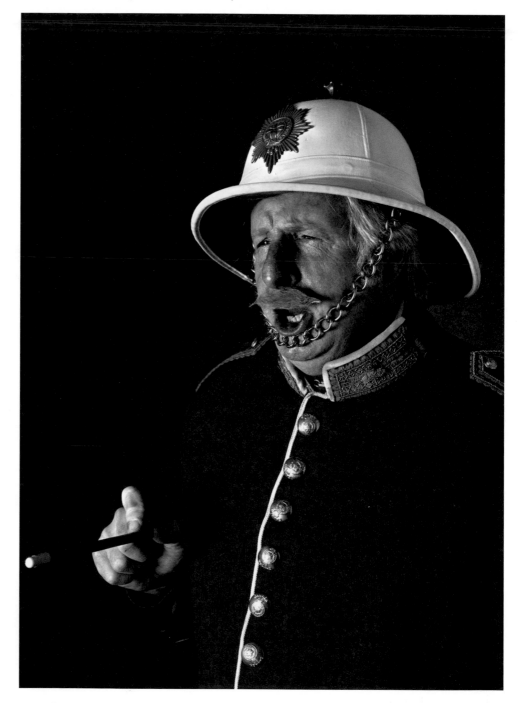

with the Mayor greeting the crowds.

Liverymen still wear traditional dress on special occasions. An example is the Dyers' and Vintners' Companies, who, arrayed in scarlet uniforms, take to the boats for "Swan Upping" on the River Thames.

The Queen's Swan Marker and the members use six traditional rowing skiffs, each flying appropriate flags and pennants. Upping takes five days. Passing Windsor Castle, the whole company stands to attention in the boats and salutes the "Seigneur of the Swans." Unmarked swans belong to the Sovereign. The Companies' swans have a sign on the beak. This was important when swans were eaten, and nowadays this seemingly silly custom has a very serious purpose: it provides a census of the numbers and health of birds on the river. Young birds are examined and weighed.

Modern companies are founded with occupations unimaginable to medieval craftsmen — Airline Pilots and Navigators, Scientific Instrument Makers, and World Traders. Each company has its own coat of arms.

In America, organizations such as the Screen Actors Guild and the Writers Guild of America are in the same tradition of a body of workers with special expertise.

ROD AND STAFF

Rods, sticks, staffs, and scepters represent power. Men have maces, scepters, croziers, a baton to conduct an orchestra, or a staff of office.

Maces were originally weapons, but now they are usually highly decorative and made of precious metals. They symbolize authority — royal, judicial, political, and religious.

One of the most famous sticks is held by the Gentleman Usher of the Black Rod, a post established in 1350. The rod is of ebony with a gold lion on the top.

At the state opening of the British Parliament, he is sent to summon the House of Commons to hear the Queen's speech in the House of Lords. The doors of the Commons are symbolically slammed in his face, showing the Common's independence from the sovereign. He has to hammer on the doors with his rod to be admitted.

Egyptian pharaohs are shown smiting their enemies with maces. Two other symbols of the authority of pharaoh or deities are the crook and flail. The crook is a shepherd's staff, and is echoed in the croziers carried by bishops and archbishops. The bishop is a good shepherd to his flock, with his crook to pull strays back into the fold.

Over history, the lingam has been worshipped in India. It is a symbol of Lord Siva, the Hindu deity, and is a symbol of the transmission of life. Lord Krishna's flute is very similar.

Women have few sticks that, like the broomstick and wand, often have a negative connotation.

His rod and staff are to punish and lead the flock and to goad them toward the right path.

The regalia of Hindu kings included a *danda*, or staff. *Dandas* are common in Indian and Pakistan, carried by policemen and used to enforce orders, punish, chastise, and control.

ABOVE: The British army have pace sticks, used originally to pace guns, but later used to measure the pace of soldiers — to ensure precision marching during ceremonies.

LEFT: Lord Krishna enchants with his flute.

FAR LEFT: A policeman in Mumbai, India with his lathi, a staff for law enforcement.

OPPOSITE: Flail and crook shown in a painting in the tomb of Queen Nefertari, Luxor, Egypt.

TRADE AND BUSINESS

In Roman times, the sign for a tavern was a small cut tree placed above the door. In Medieval England few people were literate, so many businesses had signs, and in 1393 a law was passed making it compulsory for publicans to have inn signs.

Inn names, and the signs designed to illustrate them, come from a wide variety of sources. Many, like The Malt Shovel, or The Bricklayer's Arms, signify local trades. Others refer to historic events — The Royal Oak, The Rose and Crown. Uncommon names sometimes require an understanding of symbology. The Bag o' Nails in Bristol, England, traditionally considered a haunt of carpenters, probably derives from the word "bacchanal" — pertaining to Bacchus, the god of wine.

The sad tale of Dirty Dicks in London is of an ironmonger whose bride died on the eve of the wedding. The inconsolable groom never washed or changed his clothes again, and when his cats died he left the corpses where they were. It is said he was the model for Miss Havisham in Dicken's *Great Expectations*. His shop was later opened as a pub, with all of his possessions (dead cats included) on

BUCKET of BLOOD

display, but never fear — you can drink there safely as it was cleaned up in the 19th century.

Pubs with two ill-matched names such as The Red Lion and Pineapple, often represented two original establishments that have since merged.

Names that include the word "three" — Three Horseshoes, Three Tuns — often relate to livery companies — in these cases the Worshipful Companies of Farriers and Brewers and Vintners.

The Elephant and Castle is usually claimed to refer to the Infanta (princess) of Castille, fiancée of King Charles I. More probably it relates to the

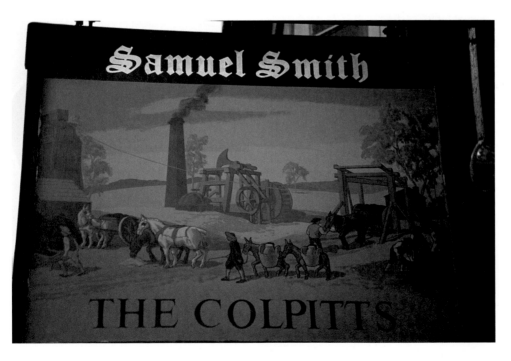

LEFT: Dirty Dicks in the City of London.

OPPOSITE LEFT: The Colpitts reflects the local mining industry of Durham in the northeast of England.

OPPOSITE RIGHT: The Bucket of Blood is at Hayle, Cornwell. A pub for butchers or surgeons, maybe?

Worshipful Company of Cutlers, whose arms have an elephant with a castle-shaped howdah.

The First and Last Inn is naturally situated at Lands End in Cornwall, England.

Other businesses advertised their presence with specific symbols. Chemists used carboys of colored liquid in the window. The barber has a red and white striped pole. Originally barbers were barber-surgeons and kept leeches for bloodletting. The patient grasped the pole and the bandage was tied to it. When not in use, it was hung on the door and became the sign for a barber surgeon's shop.

A black doll was a sign of rag dealers. The origin is said to be a dealer who found a beautiful black doll and put it up in the hope that the owner would claim it. The pawnshop has three balls, a symbol of Lombard banking. Gloves, boots, and hat signs all advertised the relevant shops.

Many countries have signs on gable ends or in the woodwork of a building, many of which are trade signs — scissors for a tailor, a glass of gin for a publican, a ship for a ship's master.

Not all business was conducted indoors. "On the nail" means striking a bargain, and it is said that the phrase relates to bronze pillars, called "nails," found outside English and Irish stock

ABOVE: Snake and cup — an ancient symbol of healing, forming the handles of a chemist's shop in Sicily.

LEFT: Fancy bottles and carboys of colored water were the sign of a chemist's shop.

OPPOSITE ABOVE LEFT: The traditional striped pole advertises a barber's shop.

OPPOSITE ABOVE RIGHT: The three golden balls of the pawnbroker.

OPPOSITE BELOW: Felsted village sign, Essex, England.

and commodity exchanges. If a man was making a bargain, he put his money "on the nail," indicating an agreed contract.

When labor became organized in Britain, each trade union designed its own banner. Made of silk, they were beautifully painted, using images from the Bible, heraldry, newly developed socialist iconography, and popular symbols like the all-seeing eye.

The communist hammer and sickle symbol developed in about 1918. The hammer indicates their masculine energy can be used to create or destroy. Thor used a hammer both to create valleys and to kill. The sickle represents agriculture. Together, they symbolize fruitful industry and industriousness.

Villages and towns often have their own signs and crests of arms. Felsted in Essex, England, has a sign showing various aspects of the village.

The large church shows that this was a prosperous and God-fearing village. Felsted School is a major institution. Boote House (built 1596) is a local landmark. Beer barrels represent Ridley's Brewery. Sugar beet is grown and was processed locally, and wheat was another important crop. The Domesday Book shows that the village was first mentioned in 1086.

CHAPTER FOUR

RELIGIOUS SYMBOLS

Symbols were particularly important in church iconography, in order to teach the illiterate.

The apostles are often symbolized by the manner of their death. St. Andrew was crucified on a diagonal cross, so his symbol is a saltire; St. Bartholomew was flayed, symbolized by a knife; St. John is symbolized by a cup with a snake coming out of it. He was challenged to drink poison but was unharmed.

St. James the Great is associated with scallop shells and pilgrimage. These relate to the pilgrimage center of the saint at Compostella in Spain.

St. James the Less is associated with a windmill or a saw, as he was martyred with a saw. St. Jude's symbol is a ship, as he travelled as a missionary. St. Matthew was a tax collector, and is often symbolized by moneybags or a chest.

St. Peter is known by his crossed keys, and by the rooster that crowed as

recalling his death. He is sometimes given a builder's square, a reference to his building of a church in India.

St. Matthias is symbolized by a lance, which is how he met his death. Judas is not included with the

he denied Christ. St. Simon is given a fish symbol: Christ said, "I will make you fishers of men." St. Philip's sign is a long, upturned cross on which he was crucified and a basket of fish, recalling the feeding of the five thousand. St. Thomas has a lance, stones and arrows,

ABOVE: The scallop shell is associated with St. James the Great.

RIGHT: St. Sebastian is usually portrayed covered with arrows.

OPPOSITE: The Apostles on the tree of life.

LEFT: Martin Luther King at Westminster Abbey.

OPPOSITE LEFT: St. Joan of Arc often has a shield and the Croix de Lorraine.

OPPOSITE RIGHT: St. Francis of Assisi is usually associated with animals or with his stigmata.

others, but if he is symbolized it is usually with a noose or moneybag, overflowing with the silver he received for Christ's betrayal.

The Apostles' Creed, a statement of belief, is considered a symbol of the apostles.

The four evangelists are symbolized as the four creatures that surround the Throne of God: St. Matthew's symbol is a human or angel; St. Mark's symbol is a lion; St. Luke has an ox; and St. John an eagle.

Numerous saints also have symbols. St. Christopher carried the Christchild on his shoulders and takes care of travelers. St. Sebastian was extremely popular in early art, and is shown bristling with the arrows that caused his martyrdom.

On the west front of Westminster

Abbey in London, Dr. Martin Luther King lacks symbols, apart from the child "for whom he had a dream." In an age of literacy, his name is enough.

THE CROSS

The cross is a universal symbol. It is the Axis Mundi around which everything revolves, the center of the cosmos, the tree of life, Jacob's ladder, a link between heaven and earth. It symbolizes both passion and forgiveness.

Ornate, carved crosses were erected long before churches existed, often sited on pagan shrines. The Puritans destroyed many of them.

Thought to have originated in Ireland in the 8th century, Celtic crosses are strong and ringed. Early examples had geometric motifs. By the 9th and 10th centuries there were Biblical scenes. None dates from after the 12th century.

Muiredach's Cross in Ireland is considered the finest, and displays two cats on the base, one with a kitten and the other with a bird. Above, there are

RIGHT: The Eleanor Cross at Hardingstone, Northamptonshire, England is one of three that still survive intact.

BELOW: Muiredach's Cross at Monasterboice, Ireland, is arguably the finest of the Celtic high crosses.

OPPOSITE: Jacob's ladder — seen by Christians as bridging the gap between earth and heaven, from the Church of St. Peter and St. Paul, Chaldon, Surrey, England.

Biblical scenes — Adam and Eve, Cain and Abel, Moses, Samson, David and Goliath. The reverse shows the life of Christ — the flight into Egypt, the baptism, Christ mocked, and the tomb. Another scene shows two men pulling each other's beards.

Memorial crosses are found all over the world. One of the oldest is over 1,000 years old, erected by monks from Lindisfarne fleeing the Danes with the body of St. Cuthbert. Charing Cross in London is one site on the route of the coffin of Eleanor of Castile, wife of Edward I, from Nottinghamshire to Westminster Abbey.

The police in Arizona began planting white crosses at sites of fatalities in the 1940s and 1950s and although they then stopped, relatives continue to place such memorials.

In America, Britain, and Australia many little roadside shrines are seen, memorials to those who have died in accidents — sometimes a wooden cross, sometimes just a bunch of flowers, still wrapped in plastic. Probably the largest such collections were devoted to Diana, Princess of Wales.

ABOVE LEFT: Flowers placed at the site of an accident.

LEFT: Tributes to Diana, Princess of Wales.

OPPOSITE LEFT: People give thanks for blessings received.

OPPOSITE RIGHT: A collection of ex votos at Samos, Greece.

VOTIVES, EX VOTOS, AND MILAGROS

The idea of leaving a symbol at a shrine is very ancient and universal. Iron Age men sacrificed valuable weapons, such as fine swords, as votive offerings. Mesoamericans had a similar custom. All over the Indian sub-continent special trees are covered with ties — scraps of cloth torn from the garments of people who have asked the resident goddess for aid.

An ex voto (*ex voto suscepto* – "from the vow made") is a symbol of

gratitude to a saint or divinity to whom a vow or request has been made. Ex votos are often small model legs, arms, hearts, eyes, and other body parts, symbolizing the relevant affliction. Apart from thanks they provide hope to others. The symbols are often made of gold or silver, but they can be tin. In Fatima, Portugal, it was common to give a wax cast of a body part and in Mexico paintings are often made illustrating the problem. In ancient Greece, tablets were prepared and placed in shrines as votive offerings, often to Persephone and Aphrodite. Sumerians left large-eyed votive statues, perhaps symbolizing themselves, in their temples. They are thought to have prayed for them. The Romans deposited large numbers of symbolic objects at the hot springs of the goddess Aquae Sulis in the English town of Bath. They were seeking help with ailments. But the items they deposited were not all kindly: there was a custom of placing curse tablets, wishing ill to enemies.

Many European churches have model ships donated by those who survived dangers at sea. These are most common in the ports of the Hanseatic League (a 13th- to 17th-century northern European alliance of trading

guilds). Notre Dame de Boulogne in the French port of Boulogne-sur-Mer, has a collection of them.

The Church of Gesù Nuove in Naples, Italy, has a chapel dedicated to Guiseppe Moscali (1880–1927), a local doctor who was canonized in 1977. His entire study is recreated in the church, including the chair in which he died. Ex votos include the usual range of body parts and golden syringes. Carved markings on the outside of the church are said by some to be inverted esoteric signs that have cursed the building. In Naples there was a custom of giving gold and silver ex votos to deceased poor people, in return for small favors in the afterlife.

Migrants took the custom to churches in North America. Many churches around the world have racks for votive candles. Light one, and say a prayer.

In some places, larger items are left. Lourdes has crutches and walking aids. The Duomo in Siena, Italy, has a wall of helmets placed there by grateful people who survived motorcycle accidents.

Milagros (the word means "miracle" or "surprise") are similar to ex votos, but are often given before the event, as a request for help. They are similar body

parts and animals, fruit, and vegetables. In Latin America such symbols can be bought and used as amulets or talismans, or given to others in the hope that the symbol may cure their ailments and solve their problems.

OPPOSITE: Votive lights at Les Saintes Marie de la Mer, Camargue, France.

CHAPTER FIVE
THE WORLD, CALENDARS & TIME

AXIS MUNDI

The Axis Mundi, the center of the world, is a symbol representing a point of connection between earth and the heavens, offering a means of travel between the two realms.

It is the point where the world began: in some cultures called Eden. Here all directions meet and the treasures of heaven may be spread across the world.

The Axis Mundi can also be seen as a natural object, often a mountain like Mount Fuji in Japan. The Himalayan Mount Kailash is revered by several Indian religions.

The Axis also can be a building — the Kaaba in Mecca, the Dome of the Rock in Jerusalem, the ziggurats of Mesopotamia, or the pyramids of Teotihuacán.

Trees are symbols of the Axis because their branches stretch to the sky, trunks meet the earth, and roots

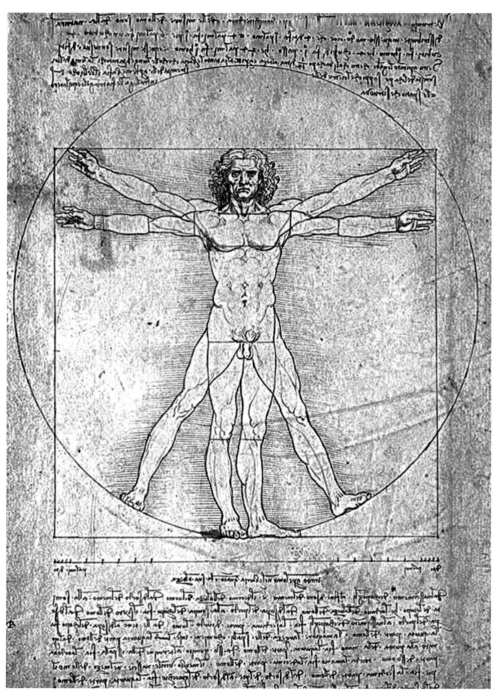

push into the underworld. Sometimes, trees of life are represented as upside down, with the roots in heaven and branches disseminating wisdom on earth. Many cultures have the symbol

ABOVE: The Dome of the Rock in Jerusalem is an Axis Mundi in Islamic belief.

RIGHT: Leonardo Da Vinci's Vitruvian Man, demonstrating the mathematics of man as an Axis Mundi.

OPPOSITE: To the Sioux the Axis is the Black Hills of Dakota.

OPPOSITE: Modern skyscrapers are symbolic centers of the world: downtown Dallas from the Reunion Tower.

RIGHT: Aztec Sun God calendar — the stone of five suns.

of a tree of life or a world tree. Banyan and Bodhi trees (the tree under which Buddha was enlightened) are valued in India. Yggdrasil is the Nordic tree, linking the nine worlds of Norse cosmology.

Some have linked the Sefiroth of the Cabala with the tree of life. This tree in the Cabala is the map of creation and cosmology. The symbol also mirrors the human body.

CALENDAR

Many cultures have their own calendar, dating from a significant event. The Indians, Chinese, Muslims, and Jews all start their calendars in different years. In India, metal perpetual calendars allow the calculation of festivals.

Mesoamerican calendars date back to the sixth century BCE, used by Zatopecs and Olmecs and later developed by the Maya and Aztecs, experts in astronomy. The calendars are based on the earth's rotation around the sun. The Pleiades constellation is significant as indicating the start of the Aztec year.

The Aztec calendar or sunstone is a symbol of Mexico. It dates from the 15th century CE. The face of the sun God is at the center and rings encircle him, symbolizing periods, days, and events in the natural world. The Aztec universe is reflected in the stone. Aztecs had a 365-day year divided into eighteen 20-day months. Five days were left for new year festivities. Thirteen days were devoted to specific gods who influenced the mood of the day.

The Mayans had two calendars. The first described a solar year of 256 days, which was used for domestic life, planting, and harvesting. The second, or the Tzolkin, was a 260-day calendar for ritual uses. Birth charts would be drawn up for baby boys calculating whether the individual should be a soldier, priest, or sacrificial victim. A 584-day Venus cycle was also important, as Venus was also considered inauspicious and therefore associated with warfare and unpleasant events.

The Inca calendar accurately followed the movement of the sun, vital for agriculture. Temples were aligned allowing the sun's light to fall at a particular place during equinoxes and solstices, such as the "Hitching Post of the Sun" at Machu Picchu. At midday on the equinoxes the sun was directly above the "post," and therefore left no shadow. The Incas based their calendar on observations of the sun, moon, and stars, and had twelve months related to agriculture and festivals.

LEFT: An Indian perpetual calendar.

OPPOSITE: At Chichen Itza, Mexico, the Chac Mool is a receptacle for hearts sacrificed to the Mayan rain god.

In Islam, the lunar calendar is used to calculate festival days, but it is not useful for agriculture, so other calendars are also used. The Chinese have a lunar calendar, and Hindus take into account both lunar and solar months; there are also several regional calendars and calendars observed by different sects.

Calendars are so important in India that key rings often carry a metal perpetual calendar enabling calendrical calculations to be made.

CLOCKS — SIGNS OF THE TIME

Mankind has always been eager to mark the time and many of the earliest efforts to do so were in the form of sundials.

Throughout history sundials have been inscribed with mottos, often in Latin. *Tempus fugit*, "time flies" is a common inscription.

Early clocks did not have dials — they just struck the hours. Few could have read them anyway. The oldest public clock dates from 1386, and is still working in Salisbury Cathedral.

LEFT & OPPOSITE: Salisbury Cathedral in southern England has an ancient clock that is still working.

OPPOSITE: Le Gros Horloge in Rouen, France has only one hand — who needs minutes?

Old clocks often had a "clockjack," a human figure who struck a bell marking the quarter hours. Such figures can be seen at Wells and Norwich Cathedrals, England. Wells has two of them: one indoors and one outside.

Le Gros Horloge in Rouen, Normandy, dates from 1389, and has one hand (no one needed minutes in those days). However, it has a half-black, half-silver ball to tell the moon's phases, and it also marks the days of the week. This was important information for an agricultural society. It has representations of the planets, and of the sun god Apollo.

The Orloj in Prague, an astronomical clock, is an object of beauty with its shining hands and delicate wheels. It has an astrological dial and a ring indicating the current position within the zodiac. It is flanked by four figures — Death, symbolized by a skeleton who strikes the hours; Pride, a figure holding a mirror; Greed, who is holding a bag of money; and a Turk,

who wears a turban.

By the eighteenth century, worldwide exploration and trade made accurate time keeping the goal of many a clockmaker. John Harrison's famous marine chronometer proved its enormous accuracy on a voyage in 1761. Sailors could now measure local time, but they also needed a reference point, which was established as the Greenwich meridian, to calculate their exact longitude.

Harrison's chronometer saved many lives and vessels, and was an immense aid to trade and travel.

ABOVE: The Greenwich meridian line in London is marked on the ground: you can have one foot in the eastern hemisphere and the other in the west.

RIGHT: Stonehenge — is this the most ancient clock of all? Its stones are aligned to sunrise in midwinter and midsummer.

CHAPTER SIX
FERTILITY, FIGUREHEADS & FIRE

Fertility symbols surround us; indeed, many of them have become clichés. Spring is a time when fertility is at its height and the world is reborn, with baby animals everywhere. The story goes that a goddess once saved a frozen bird by turning it into a rabbit. The creature could still lay eggs; hence the Easter Bunny was born, a character who manages to combine two fertility symbols — eggs and rabbits. Eggs are seen as life-giving and have long been an Eastern Orthodox symbol. Popular with the

Russian ruling house, they were sometimes made of precious metals and richly ornamented. Painted porcelain eggs were also very popular.

The Venus of Willendorf is an example of an early fertility symbol.

SHEELA-NA-GIGS

Sheela-na-Gigs are found in Ireland, England, France, and Spain, and in lesser numbers in other European countries from Norway to the Czech Republic. They are found in areas of Anglo-Norman conquest, usually (but not exclusively) on churches. They show a female form.

We do not know exactly what they symbolize. Since there are so many of them, it is reasonable to suppose that they served a specific purpose for the Medieval church. They are unlikely to be magical or sacrilegious. They may be morality figures. This is the most rational explanation,

RIGHT: A Green Man, a later Medieval carving in the Quire at Winchester Cathedral, England.

OPPOSITE LEFT: Easter Bunnies.

OPPOSITE: This decorated Russian egg remainds us of the true meaning of Easter.

as Sheela-na-Gigs often appear with other related motifs, including the Green Men, priapic figures, mermaids, centaurs, and what are known as "beard pullers" and "tongue stickers." Perhaps the most famous Sheela-na-Gig is that at Kilpeck Church on the English-Welsh border. A male and female were recently discovered at Devizes in Wiltshire.

A further candidate for a huge fertility symbol can be found not far from Devizes — Stonehenge. Anthony Perks of the University of British Colombia claims that the giant stone circle at the heart of the monumental

BELOW: Feed the cat the tradition says, and the sun will shine on your marriage.

OPPOSITE LEFT: Sheela-na-Gig, Kilpeck Church, Herefordshire, England.

RIGHT: Coconuts are an Indian fertility symbol.

lanscape is a symbol of the feminie.

INDIA

The Indian Jains induce fertility by singing ancient lullabies and swinging an ancient cradle. This is particularly effective at the time of celebrations of the birth of Mahavira, a revered figure who achieved enlightenment and shows others the way. Coconuts are another important Indian fertility symbol.

SCANDINAVIA

Cats are sacred to Freyja, the Scandinavian love goddess, whose chariot is pulled by cats. It is said of the bride whom the sun shines on that "she has fed the cat well," so the marriage should be fruitful and successful.

NORTH AMERICA

The sun, stars, and the crescent moon are regarded as fertility symbols by some North American native groups. Dragonflies, frogs, and tadpoles symbolize spring, water, and fertility, with tadpoles regarded as particularly powerful because of the way they change from frogspawn to fully developed frog.

In New Mexico and Colorado a bent old man called Kokopelli is a seed bringer and water sprinkler.

CORN DOLLIES

Corn dollies are made to ensure continuity from one fertile harvest to another. Usually made from the last corn to be cut, they come in many shapes, not all of which are doll-like. They are made all over Europe. In Montenegro, a doll dressed as a rich lady was to encourage the harvest.

In Bali the dolly is the likeness of a goddess made of plaited, ripened grain and she is to be kept until next harvest, to stave off disasters, floods, drought, and blight.

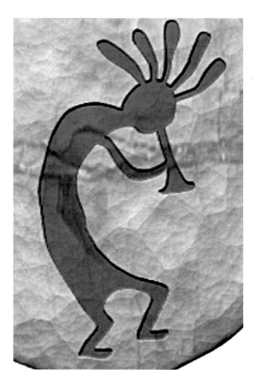

FERTILITY, FIGUREHEADS & FIRE

LEFT: *Krishna, the Indian deity, with his flute.*

BELOW: *A beautifully dressed corn dolly from Latvia.*

OPPOSITE LEFT: *Kokopelli attracts women with his flute.*

OPPOSITE RIGHT: *Dragonflies symbolize the coming of spring.*

SUPERNATURAL SIGNS, SYMBOLS, AND CODES

FIGUREHEADS

Romans, Greeks, and Vikings all had figureheads on their boats. The Vikings often carved dragons or snakes.

Many of the figureheads on ships between the 16th and 19th centuries were of women. American female figureheads were likely modeled on the wives of ship owners.

They were often symbolic, a means of identification for largely illiterate people. The carvings were highly individualistic, and sometimes related to superstitions and religious ideas. Some compare them to the soul of the ship, a divine figure who prevented

BELOW: Replica of a Viking ship.

OPPOSITE ABOVE: The preserved hull of the Mary Rose, *the flagship of King Henry VIII, rescued from Portsmouth harbor.*

OPPOSITE BELOW: Nannie, the figurehead from the Cutty Sark, *fortunately escaped the fire.*

London, and undergoing repair having suffered a serious fire, has a figurehead called "Nannie." The name *Cutty Sark* relates to the Scottish tale of Tam o' Shanter, who saw a witch dancing in a short skirt. These skirts were called cutty sarks. The witch pursued Tam and pulled off his horse's tail. Nannie holds nothing, though sailors used to make tails of rope and put them in her hands. Presumably the ship was named to emulate the speed of the witch, symbolized in Nannie. The clipper *Tweed*'s figurehead was the head of Tam o' Shanter, and the *Styx* had a full length devil on her bow. The diva

shipwreck, or in the case of sinking led the souls of the dead to comfort. Animals were also popular, with the lion a frequent choice, especially when there were royal connections. The *Mary Rose*, Henry VIII's famous warship, had a unicorn.

Pirates and privateers had their own ideas for figureheads — Captain Death had a skeleton, Cap'n Jack Sparrow's *Black Pearl* had a beautiful woman, arm held up, with a bird taking flight from her hand.

The famous tea clipper, the *Cutty Sark,* now docked at Greenwich,

OPPOSITE: A replica of the Golden Hind *in Brixham Harbor, Devon, England*

BELOW: The Golden Hind*'s figurehead is a gilded deer.*

RIGHT: The Cutty Sark.

BELOW RIGHT: The ship's anchor is a sign of hope, patience, and steadfastness.

Jenny Lind, the "Swedish nightingale," was the model for the figurehead of another clipper, the *Nightingale*.

Some figureheads were royal portraits. William III's *Britannia* had the royal arms as a figurehead, together with related heraldic devices.

One unfortunate figurehead was that of HMS *Atlas*. The figurehead was

129

too tall and had to be sawn to fit. This necessitated sawing off the top of the globe — with it, it is said, went the American colonies. As this happened in 1782 during the war of American Independence, it was seen as a bad omen.

Figureheads were often beautifully carved and carefully planned with immense symbolic significance. American ones made use of mythological characters, allegorical figures, and national emblems and symbols. Later, they used political figures. The U.S. frigate *Constitution* had Hercules, who was later replaced by Neptune, then in 1833 Neptune was replaced by Andrew Jackson. This caused some dispute, so it was sawn off and then secretly replaced.

There is nowhere on most ships to attach a figurehead now, but many still have a metal badge carrying appropriate symbols.

ABOVE: An anchor on a memorial to those who died at sea, Ave Maria Stella, Gironde Estuary, France.

OPPOSITE: USS Constitution, *"Old Ironsides," in Boston Harbor, Massachusetts, USA.*

FIRE AND FLAMES

Fires symbolize purification, consecration, and lighting the darkness of winter.

Fire can create intense emotion if a national emblem such as a flag is burned.

Beacons are lit on hilltops in Britain to signal important events — nowadays celebrations rather than warnings. Formerly, they warned of danger like the arrival of the Spanish Armada in 1577.

Lord Macaulay captured the drama:

And on, and on, without a pause,
untired they bounded still
All night from tower to tower they
sprang; they sprang from hill to hill.

In 1455, the Scots passed a law to use beacons to warn of the approaching English. One fire meant that you believed they were on the way, two meant that they were certain, and four

RIGHT: Running with burning barrels at Ottery St. Mary, England, on Bonfire Night.

OPPOSITE: Burning a Viking longship at Up Helly Aa, Lerwick, Shetland Isles.

fires meant that the English were coming in large numbers.

It was the same in Wales — the Brecon Beacons have specific fire sites. There is even a town called Beacon in the Fishkill Mountains of New York State where fires were lit to warn when the British were coming!

Many countries have a traditional time for bonfires. In Britain it is the 5th of November, recalling the plot to blow up the king and government in 1605. Both Samuel Pepys and John Evelyn refer to bonfires in their diaries.

Lewis, the county town of East Sussex, England is a center for

OPPOSITE: Jack O'Lantern carved from a pumpkin is Halloween's light.

RIGHT: Zoroastrian Fire Temple in Azerbaijan.

bonfires, held on November 5th every year. There are processions through the streets in extraordinary fancy dress, carrying seventeen burning crosses, symbolizing seventeen local Protestant martyrs killed by Mary Tudor between 1555 and 1557. "Enemies of bonfire" (politicians and unpopular public figures) are burned on bonfires, while wreaths of poppies symbolizing the dead in Flanders and other wars are laid at the war memorial.

Men, women, and children run down the streets of Ottery St. Mary, Devon, with burning tar barrels weighing 66 lbs. (30 kg) on their backs.

At the other end of the country, in Up Helly Aa in Lerwick is the main town of the Shetland Islands. It has another torchlight procession that ends with the burning of a replica Viking long ship. The Viking ship is the symbol of modern Shetland, and is found on its coat of arms.

Wiccans burn nine different kinds of wood for the celebration of Beltane or May Day — birch for the goddess and energy; oak for the god and the masculine; hazel for knowledge and wisdom; rowan for life; hawthorn for purity; willow for death; fir for birth and rebirth; apple for love and family; and the vine for strength and unity.

Fire is a major symbol in several religious faiths. Zoroastrians revere fire and see it as a symbol of righteousness and truth.

Many Hindu rituals involve fire.

Arati is performed several times a day and consists of waving ritual lights, wicks soaked in ghee, before deities. This wards off evil from both people and the deities. *Yajna*, a fire sacrifice, can last for a few hours or for years. Oblations are performed and coconuts, ghee, sandalwood, and other items are put into the flames. A *homa* or *havan* is performed and fruit, flowers, and cloth may be added to the flames. This ceremony is performed in honor of Agni, god of fire, who is seen as an important witness to a proper marriage. The *havan* purifies the worshipper, ensuring that any spirits in the vicinity will be burned away. It is an appropriate ceremony for a wedding, when the couple walk around the fire, or for birth, starting school, and other important occasions. It brings health and happiness, good luck, and prosperity.

FIREMARKS

Firemarks came into use in Britain following the great fire of London in 1666, in which thirteen thousand houses, and 89 churches (including St. Paul's Cathedral) were destroyed. There was no insurance in those days and fire-fighting arrangements were haphazard. The earliest insurance companies operated their own team of firefighters, but they would only tackle the fires of the firm's clients. As there were few street signs, and no house numbers, it made it necessary to have a mark fixed to the houses that were insured by a particular company. From 1680 the Phoenix Insurance Company attached marks showing a phoenix rising from the flames on theirs clients' houses.

LEFT: Arati is a ritual to ward off evil.

OPPOSITE: The Firemark on a house was an insurance policy.

Eventually, there were about 200 companies operating in London, with over 800 different marks.

Early marks were made of lead; later ones of copper and iron. The Sun Fire Office's mark was very common — naturally the symbol was a sun; the Protector Insurance Company's mark showed a fireman fighting a blaze. Characters from myths were popular.

Some careful people had more than one mark.

Firemarks were also found in Europe, Russia, and the USA.

CHAPTER SEVEN
PLANTS, FOOD &
THE NATURAL WORLD

FLOWERS

Shakespeare had Ophelia say it with flowers:

> *There's rosemary, that's for*
> *remembrance; pray, love, remember: and*
> *there is pansies. That's for thoughts.*
> *There's fennel for you, and columbines:*
> *there's rue for you; and here's some for*
> *me: we may call it herb-grace o'*
> *Sundays: O you must wear your rue with*
> *a difference. There's a daisy: I would give*
> *you some violets, but they withered all*
> *when my father died: they say he made a*
> *good end, —*

Ophelia distributes her posy to symbolize events: her brother Laertes gets rosemary and pansies, for remembrance, thoughts, and faithfulness.

Fennel and columbine go to the king, fennel symbolizing flattery, deceit, and infidelity. Columbine is an emblem of deceived lovers and symbolizes

ingratitude and faithlessness. The symbolic language of the flowers is capable of making a stronger statement than mere words.

Rue goes to the queen, who must wear it "with a difference." Ophelia's rue speaks of tears for the loss of a father; Gertrude's rue "worn with a difference" shows sorrow and contrition, she should feel guilt. Rue is very bitter and was used to cause miscarriages, so it was linked to adultery.

The innocent daisy Ophelia puts down and leaves, and there are no violets, so innocence, faithfulness, and integrity are lacking here.

In *A Winter's Tale*, Perdita regrets not having spring flowers and gives midsummer blooms to suit the morals and age of middle-aged recipients: hot lavender, mints, savory, marjoram, and marigolds.

The Victorians had their language of flowers, creating bouquets symbolizing deepest feelings — true love and passion expressed in a handful of blooms. It

OPPOSITE: Ophelia's pansies would have been today's small violas.

RIGHT: Innocence perfectly symbolized — the daisy.

must have been cutting to receive a bouquet of withered flowers, symbolizing rejection. For the truly spiteful, there are flowers with unflattering meanings. Aloe, evening primrose, meadowsweet, petunia, hydrangea, and foxglove would translate as grief, inconstancy, uselessness, resentment and anger, frigidity and heartlessness, and insincerity.

The green carnation was associated with Oscar Wilde. Nowadays, passionflowers are associated with the gay community.

It was the custom to have funeral garlands in many lands. In Europe, these were particularly made for unmarried women who had died. White lilies were placed on the graves of young and innocent people. Bridal flowers and scattered petals are probably universal.

It might be worth considering that

OPPOSITE LEFT: It only remains to add a cyclamen, meaning "goodbye."

OPPOSITE RIGHT: Tulips and flowers of the field are suitably colorful for Sagittarians.

LEFT: Pisces should be sent tranquil blue and indigo flowers; forget-me-nots are especially recommended.

astrology can also be used in selecting suitable flowers. Vivid blooms represent Aries, such as scarlet roses or showy tulips.

Countries and states often have floral symbols. India has the lotus, a bloom also associated with creation and the Hindu gods. Lakshmi and Brahma are seated on lotus blossom thrones. It symbolizes purity, floating above the muddy waters of attachment and desire.

The comedy troupe Monty Python produced the lines "This here's the yellow wattle, the emblem of our land, you can stick it in a bottle, you can hold it in your hand," and with this in mind, many will never forget the Australian flower. The Australian sporting colors, yellow and green, echo the symbol.

The meaning of flowers is

considered rarely these days. Perhaps we should think much harder when choosing flowers for special occasions: some blossoms could be inappropriate.

HERBS

Ovid said, "Medicine sometimes grants health, sometimes destroys it, showing which plants are helpful, which do harm."

Dioscorides (1st century CE) was from modern Turkey. He was well

traveled and an expert in the use of herbs, animal products, and minerals as medicines. His *Materia Medica* was the basis of pharmacology until the 16th century. He researched the physiological effect of medicine on the body. Herbals were copied and written in many Islamic countries.

From ancient times until the 19th century, men believed that the humors controlled health. There were four humors: black bile, associated with melancholic; yellow bile, associated with choleric; phlegm, associated with phlegmatic; and blood, associated with sanguine. As long as the humors were balanced, everything was fine, but if

ABOVE RIGHT: An Arabic herbal book from the Topkapi Palace in Istanbul shows the details of plants and exquisite calligraphy.

RIGHT: Basil thriving in a Greek monastery.

OPPOSITE LEFT: The goddess Lakshmi seated on a lotus flower.

OPPOSITE RIGHT: The yellow wattle symbolizes Australia and the colors are worn by her sportsmen.

they became unbalanced, health and personality suffered. This theory was used as a basis for treatment, deciding whether to bleed or purge the patient. Medicine was often herbal, but consideration of the humors, zodiac, and "signatures" was vital. Paracelsus was a "doctor of signatures," and used plants that bore resemblance to body parts to effect a cure.

In the 16th and 17th centuries "physick" gardens appeared. Culpeper's *Herbal,* of 1652, was a great collection of possible cures, using English plants. Culpeper quoted Dioscorides, and associated planets with herbs. The doctor treated the patient using plants governed by opposing planets or, sometimes, sympathetic ones. Herbs governed by Venus alleviated women's problems.

OPPOSITE: Here, in a reenactment of the Battle of Hastings, in Sussex, England, "medieval herbalists" offer cures.

RIGHT: Marigolds symbolized enduring love.

Culpeper saw basil as a herb of Mars and under the sign of the scorpion, sometimes called "basilicon." It was good for venomous stings and bites and helped women to recover after giving birth, "and as it helps the deficiency of Venus in one kind, so it spoils her in another. I dare write no more of it."

Many Indian families have a basil plant in their courtyard. It is a symbol of the god Vishnu. It is carefully tended and watered, and a lamp is lit in the evenings at the altar. Cultures regard basil variously: in Italy it symbolizes love; in Ancient Greece, hate. In European folklore it was a symbol of Satan.

Thyme symbolized sacrifice and courage, and was often embroidered onto gifts for crusaders. Lavender was associated with laundry, and so associated with purity and virtue. Chamomile symbolized humility, and marigold, enduring love. Garlic (handy

OPPOSITE: Chamomile symbolized humility.

RIGHT: Lavender was associated with purity and virtue. Lavender fields in Provence, France.

to repel vampires) symbolized the cosmos, having many layers.

Noble families were associated with particular herbs and plants. The Plantagenets' emblem, from which they took their name, was genera *Genista*, the broom. It grows on the mound of Henry II's tower at Windsor.

FRUIT

Fruit as a symbol varies according to different cultures.

The apricot is a symbol for the skin. For the Chinese, the peach symbolizes springtime, marriage, fertility, and long life. For a Christian it symbolizes virtue and truth. The luscious cherry symbolizes beauty and sexuality.

Apples are very common symbols. "An apple a day keeps the doctor away" is to safeguard health and grant

OPPOSITE: Fruit is good to eat and rich in symbolism.

RIGHT: Apricots are symbols for the skin.

BELOW: Cherries are for beauty.

immortality. The "apple of your eye" is your beloved.

Quinces and pears are associated with virtue and with fertility. The Ancient Greeks gave the bride a quince to ensure the marriage was fruitful.

Raspberries are kindness in

LEFT: A fertile quince tree with delicious fruit.

BELOW: The walnut was considered suitable for brain medicine due to its brain-like appearance.

OPPOSITE LEFT: The tomato is a symbol of revolution or disapproval.

OPPOSITE RIGHT: Pineapples on buildings were a sign of wealth; Dunmore, near Aith, Scotland.

Christian art, but used by the English and Cherokees to ease labor.

The outward appearance of fruit, leaves, and flowers was once taken as a "signature," indicative of the properties of the item. Thus, a walnut, which was wrinkly like a brain, was seen as suitable brain medicine, and liverwort,

which has a three-lobed leaf like the shape of the liver, is medicine for that organ.

The tomato was a culinary symbol of the French Revolution: it arrived in the country at the right time and it was revolutionary red. It is also symbolic of disapproval, if thrown at actors, and fun to wallow in at southern European festivals.

A pineapple is a symbol of hospitality. On houses and railings in London, it is a sign of wealth — "We can afford such exotic things!" A mango tells of love.

Pomegranates are reputed to have 613 seeds, symbolizing the 613 commandments in the Torah.

TREES

A tree stood at the center of the Garden of Eden — the tree of the knowledge of good and evil. The tree of life is a symbol shared by many cultures. The roots are in the underworld, the trunk comes from earth and pushes up into the world, and the branches reach out to heaven. In some cases, the branches support heaven, like Yggdrassil, the Norse World Ash, or the Mayan tree. The Assyrian tree was stylized and ornamental, symbolizing the cosmic

LEFT: Pomegranates have too many seeds to count.

RIGHT: A beautiful tree adorns Wazir Khan's mosque in Lahore, India.

connection between water, earth, and sky. The Maya tree symbolizes the creation and world order. The Islamic tree symbolizes abundance and plenty; it has jewels in the branches and milk and honey springing from the roots. All of them show that humans can ascend from lower nature to achieve spiritual

ABOVE:Yggdrasil, the tree that overshadowed the world in Norse mythology.

RIGHT: Hagadah Passover cover with the tree of life.

153

LEFT: The Bodhi tree at the Mahabodhi Temple, Bodhgaya, Bihar, India.

OPPOSITE: The rowan is the Celtic tree of life and was often planted near homes and barns to protect the occupants.

knowledge and reach the heavenly connection.

The tree of life may also be upside down, the roots in heaven and the branches stretching to the earth to dispense spiritual growth. This appears in the Qabbalah and symbolized God in heaven as the source of all life, flowing down. It can be reversed "as it is above, so it is below."

Deciduous trees symbolize resurrection — apparently dead, they come to life again.

Evergreens have long been used to deck the halls. The Christmas tree was a German custom, and was believed to dispel evil. Fruit from trees is a symbol for fertility and rebirth.

Trees are special to Buddhists. The Buddha's mother leaned on a tree while in labor; the Buddha was enlightened under a Bodhi tree (and these are venerated in Asia) and he died in a grove of trees.

OPPOSITE: Hawthorn, the May Tree, is associated with love and marriage. It is unlucky to take its flowers indoors.

RIGHT: Mistletoe for a kiss at Christmas.

A tree of death is the fig that, devoid of leaf and withered, represents the opposite of life. Confusingly, it is also a symbol of plenty, religious wisdom, and immortality. Traditionally, the tree's leaves were used as covering by Adam and Eve.

A bunch of holly is said to make a man irresistible: it symbolizes death and rebirth and protects from evil. The oak is strong, loyal, long-lived, and a symbol of the life force. Its leaves bring luck, if worn, and wreaths of oak leaves were presented to Roman commanders if they were successful. The National Trust conserves land and historic houses in Britain, and uses the oak as a symbol.

Hazel represents fertility and is considered a protection against evil. The elder is a symbol of grief, mentioned by Shakespeare in *Cymbeline*. In *Love's Labours Lost* he observes Judas was hanged on it. It is associated with sorrow, death, and the cross. However, some say

that the cross was made of holly, and in Brittany the *herbe de la croix* is mistletoe.

Mistletoe is associated with the druids and is a symbol for immortality, since it thrives on its host tree and has berries in winter, when the host appears dead. There are traditions to encourage trees to fertility; one is "wassailing." Shortly after Christmas, villagers visit orchards and sing traditional songs and sprinkle cider or liquor on the roots of the trees. A less

kindly notion is that a walnut tree is more prolific if beaten. "A woman, a dog and a walnut tree, the more you beat them, the better they be."

GARDENS

In Christian tradition, it all began with a garden — Eden — symbolizing innocence. Most cultures enjoy gardens. Rocks, water, gravel, and plants are all part of the complex symbolism of Chinese and Japanese gardens. This

stems from Taoist beliefs of heaven
and earth.

Some Indian gardens are based on
mandalas, the ritual, geometric designs
that symbolize the universe, and are aids
to meditation.

Islamic gardens are precisely laid

out, the classic shape being a *char bagh* ("four garden") with four sides and four canals (symbolizing the four rivers running out of Eden, and the rivers of water, wine, milk, and honey). In India, such gardens are symbols for Hindus too, the four rivers symbolizing those running from Mount Meru.

A variation on the square could be used. The quincunx, in which points are offset by half a unit and surrounded by four others, produces the pattern of four spots on the corners and one in the center found on a di or card showing five spots. Trees in orchards were planted in the quincunx pattern. A famous example is at Cordoba, where palm trees shade interplanted orange trees. The quincunx is an alchemical symbol for the human ability to cross the four levels of physical matter (stone, plant, animals,

LEFT: Ornamental garden at the Amber fort, near Jaipur.

OPPOSITE LEFT: The Garden of Eden, the first garden of Christian tradition.

OPPOSITE RIGHT: A Hindu Mandala based on the plan of Meru with various deities and demonic beings.

and man), to reach the fifth enlightened state.

In Europe, Medieval gardens were walled, and fragrant and medicinal herbs grew among the grass. Later the knot garden became the fashion, and patterns in clipped box, creating a line with no beginning and no end, outlined spaces for planting. The knot is one of the oldest and most complex symbols, symbolizing binding and loosing, commitment, fidelity, the marriage knot, and infinity.

From the early 1700s, garden design changed radically. Fashionable and rich, well-connected, well-educated

ABOVE: Trees planted in a quincunx pattern at Santa Maria de la Cuevas, Seville, Spain.

OPPOSITE: A knot garden at the Old Palace, Hatfield, England.

intellectuals and people with artistic and architectural interests met together, and numerous symbols appeared in homes and gardens. Pyramids, obelisks, temples, and esoteric symbols from the ancient world were in harmony with the fashionable Palladian buildings. They were an expression of status and learning.

A modern Masonic garden was shown at the Royal Horticultural Society show at Tatton Park. This garden symbolizes the journey of a man from a rough stone to perfection, while traveling a path of good and evil, joy and sadness, right and wrong. A symbolic black and white path lies between the dangers of water and a verdant pasture of peace. The journey ends at a triangular seat symbolizing faith, hope, and charity, the principles of the organization. A sundial, symbol of the uncontrollable passage of time, bears the square and compasses symbol of the Freemasons.

FOOD

Food is a symbol of love, sharing, celebration, pleasure, festivals, and more. Food is a metaphor of ethnic community and gender. It is also true that everyone has a taboo against eating one food or another on religious or totemic grounds. The West is obsessed with diets. Eating together is

BELOW LEFT: This Masonic garden was designed for the Royal Horticultural Show 2006, at Tatton Park, Cheshire, England.

BELOW: Ginseng is a Chinese aphrodisiac.

OPPOSITE: The West prefers asparagus.

OPPOSITE RIGHT: Maize was central to the mythology of the Mesoamericans.

a powerful sign of acceptance and togetherness — not that we all eat the same things. Everyone consumes grain, but in different ways: sociability in the Near East means breaking bread, but in Africa and most of Europe, sociability is more likely a glass of beer! Bread in some languages is synonymous with food, and the yeast in it symbolizes transformation.

SUPERNATURAL SIGNS, SYMBOLS, AND CODES

To the Aztecs, corn (maize) was "our flesh." It is part of the creation myths of the Aztec and Mayan cultures where the first people were created from maize dough.

In India, food is offered to deities and then, as prasad, is eaten by devotees. For Sikhs, food is a powerful symbol. A special dish called *Karah Prasad* is offered in the temple before the Holy Book and is then distributed to all present.

Sikhs run communal kitchens, *langar*, at which free meals are

distributed to all. Eating together symbolizes equality and togetherness. No one knows who brought the food, or who cooked it.

ABOVE: Ladies cooking at the Gurdwara at a Sikh temple.

LEFT: A young woman takes Karah Prasad at a Sikh temple.

OPPOSITE ABOVE: A seder meal for Passover.

OPPOSITE BELOW: The Galette du Roi: *to prevent cheating, the children decide who is given each portion!*

(January 6). The galette has a small toy hidden inside and the one who finds it is king for the day and wears a paper crown.

We have party food. In Germany, gingerbread is important and *Lebkuchen* in the shape of decorated hearts, gingerbread Santa Clauses, and cakes are given to friends. Ginger is thought to have arrived in Germany in the 11th century. A more modern custom is the *hexen haus*, a gingerbread version of the cottage found by Hansel and Gretel in the story by the Brothers Grimm. Nowadays,

There can hardly be a better example of symbolic food than that eaten at Passover by Jewish families. The bitter herbs, such as horseradish and bitter lettuce, symbolize the sad lives of slaves. Horoset, a mixture of fruit, wine, and honey, symbolizes the mortar used by the slaves, and an egg symbolizes the annual sacrifice given at the Temple in Jerusalem.

The symbolism of hot cross buns is obvious. In Britain people enjoy Christmas desserts and pancakes on Pancake Day. The French make *Galette du Roi*, a special flaky-pastry apple or frangipani pie for epiphany

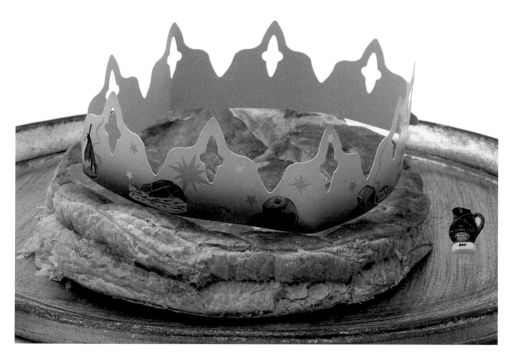

there are kits for a DIY Christmas *hexen haus*.

Some countries have seen great changes in their diets in recent times. They once ate more "slow food" — real men's heavy food like gravy, meat, and dumplings. In much of Europe, such food was a source of national pride, showing masculinity and strength. Most eastern Europeans still see this diet as a symbol of their nation but, since the fall of communism, the opening of western European hypermarkets has seen the

end of the economy of shortages and there is a much wider range available.

The result is that the masculine diet has now become more feminized — pasta, salad, and sweet dishes.
It has been said that in Poland, the emotive qualities of food symbolism drew diverse groups to focus on common grievances, overcoming divisions and creating unity against party politics.

Restaurants in parts of Europe have been transformed. Gone is the grease, the cabbage soup, and

ABOVE: A shop selling gingerbread Lebkuchen.

LEFT: The hexen haus is based on the gingerbread house from Hansel and Gretel.

OPPOSITE ABOVE: Dove of peace in a stained glass window in St. Peter's Basilica at the Vatican.

OPPOSITE BELOW: Falcon and falconer.

Dumplings. Now, gourmet dishes have arrived with a nod to tradition but cooked to current tastes.

Food is a metaphor for ethnic community and social class. Decipher the social snobbery built into the menus for a middle-class dinner party or the bill of fare at a pretentious restaurant, where food is "drizzled" and "resting on," and compare it to the traditional chamber pot full of food at old-fashioned French rural weddings.

In western Europe too, there is change. The British call the French "frogs" and, in turn, the frogs call the Brits "rosbifs." Perhaps new national stereotypes based on fast foods are needed?

NATURAL WORLD

Birds are important symbols and omens. Releasing doves is always a sign of peace, and doves symbolize true love. They represent the holy spirit, and are often found on the heraldic devices of churchmen.

A falcon, a powerful hunting bird, symbolizes majesty and power. A falcon at rest shows that the bearer is ready to carry out the service of the ruler.

Crows and ravens have a mixed reception, either being valued, or viewed as birds of ill omen, or associated with magic.

The six ravens at the Tower of London are carefully looked after by the Raven Master. Odin and Thor are among the resident birds, and Thor is a good mimic. The names are appropriate, for the Vikings often had raven symbols on their sails. If the ravens ever left the Tower, it is believed that disaster would follow.

The presence of a raven near the home or the hooting of owls is said to

foretell death. Better to have sparrows hopping about in the yard, symbolizing companionship, or a robin, symbolizing new growth.

The symbolism of birds differs from country to country. In Europe, Athena's owl symbolizes wisdom, but in northern India the owl is foolish.

Alchemists used birds to symbolize the spiritual way ahead. The black crow shows emerging consciousness and the white swan the first encounter with the etheric world. The peacock shows a turning point in inner experience of the astral world and the pelican shows sacrifice of the inner being.

PELICAN

Alchemists saw the pelican as a symbol for the formation of red stone, and an allusion to the redness of the blood of Christ. The pelican is the symbol of the Irish and Dutch blood transfusion services.

Pelicans were popular in the medieval imagination, though people had never seen one.

It was believed that a pelican would pierce its own breast to feed its young, so it symbolizes altruism — great love. The pelican was a favorite of Queen Elizabeth I. The famous portrait by Nicholas Hilliard shows the Queen wearing pearls (purity), a Tudor Rose (unity), and a pelican pendant (love).

BLUEBIRD

The happiest of symbolic birds is the bluebird, associated with anything

ABOVE: Many Medieval churches and cathedrals have pelicans. This golden pelican is in Rouen Cathedral, France.

LEFT: The phoenix speaks of the certainty of spiritual life, rising from the ashes after three days..

cheery, positive, optimistic, and joyful. In Britain during the Second World War, the song "There'll be bluebirds over the white cliffs of Dover" gladdened hearts and spread positive attitudes — in a country that has no bluebirds!

The bluebird is important to Native Americans. The Navajo saw it as a great spirit associated with the rising sun.

EAGLES

Heraldic eagles symbolize immortality, courage, far-sight, and strength. If they are double-headed or double-

tailed they are even more powerful. The eagle was associated with Zeus, Jupiter, and Odin, and was a Celtic symbol. Shamans in central Asia admired its potency and it was seen as a protector for souls ascending like birds into heaven. Charlemagne (800–814 CE) used it, and the Seljuks used an eagle with two heads, indicating interests in

ABOVE: The American bald eagle.

LEFT: The bluebird symbolizes joy and positivity.

OPPOSITE: Saraswati, goddess of wisdom, learning, and the arts, accompanied by her peacock.

Europe and Asia.

Benjamin Franklin was not impressed with the eagle design for the American Great Seal. He preferred a rattlesnake, which was more "in temper and conduct of America." Franklin didn't think highly of the bald eagle and would have preferred a turkey, a "more respectable bird." Though it was "a little vain and silly," a "Bird of Courage would not hesitate to attack a Grenadier of the British Guards who should presume to invade his farmyard with a red coat on." Anyone who has kept geese and turkeys will see the point!

PEACOCK

The peacock is a symbol of good luck, harmony, serenity, relaxation, and protection. An early Christian symbol, it can be seen in the catacombs in Rome (second century). St. Augustine was of the opinion that peacock meat does not rot, and so the belief developed that the bird symbolized eternity and eternal life. However, it was also a symbol for sin, as the bird was said to have emitted a frightful scream when it saw the ugliness of its own feet, and this is a metaphor for humans who, despite beauty, recognize

SUPERNATURAL SIGNS, SYMBOLS, AND CODES

RIGHT: The cat was sacred to Egyptians.

BELOW: A peacock in a Rajasthani fresco.

OPPOSITE ABOVE: A very large scarab at Karnak, Egypt.

OPPOSITE BELOW: Jeweled bee brooch.

(Saraswati) and wealth (Lakshmi) and the god of love (Kama). If Kama is riding a peacock, it symbolizes desire.

ANIMALS

The cat family are common in heraldry with many leopards and lions symbolizing royalty, valor, and strength. Cats were worshipped in Egypt and have never gotten over it. A black cat symbolizes good luck in the UK, but bad luck in much of the rest of Europe. It is an anarcho-syndicalist symbol, and cats were an earlier symbol for the *sans culottes* at the time of the French

their own sins. Also on the down side, it is a symbol for arrogance and vanity.

It is associated with various Indian deities, the goddesses of learning

Revolution. Their cats symbolized liberty. A dramatic black cat was the sign of *Le Chat Noir*, a bohemian cabaret in 19th-century Paris.

Heraldic bears appeared often, in the hope that the bearer would take on some of the positive qualities of the animal — its strength and cunning. It has stamina and power, warrior qualities, and its hibernation in winter speaks of resurrection. Viking berserkers wore bearskins in the hope

172

of gaining some of these qualities. Some regiments of the British Army wear bearskin caps. Native Americans shared a positive view of the bear, seeing it as strong, with humility, and a good mother and teacher.

The bee is viewed as honest, pure thinking, and with drive. The bee symbolizes industry, hard work, creativity, and diligence, and is often shown in a well-regulated hive.

The scarab or dung beetle reminded Ancient Egyptians of Khepri, self-created sun god, who wheeled the sun across the sky, like the beetle, which

they believed was self-created, wheeling his balls of dung.

Aquatic creatures make good symbols: dolphins symbolize safe travel, swiftness, charity, and love. For that reason, they were often drawn on maps.

FISH

The first incarnation (*avatar*) of the Hindu Lord Vishnu was as a fish, Matsya, who saved the world from the great flood. He is pictured with four arms, holding Vishnu's usual symbols — a conch shell (five elements), a rotating disc (mind), a gold mace (primeval

knowledge), and a lotus blossom (causal power of illusion from which the universe rises) — and he has a fish tail.

Fish are also among the eight auspicious symbols of various Indian religions. The fish can swim in the ocean of suffering, free and without fear. Being a pair, male and female,

they symbolize fertility, and some say they represent the rivers Ganges and Jumna. In China they represent unity and fidelity in marriage. In Japan they mean well-being and freedom, and carp streamers are flown like kites at a Festival for Boys, symbolizing swimming upstream and flying high,

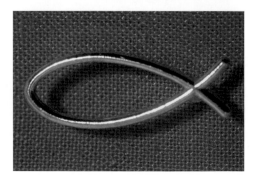

showing the boy will succeed.

The outline of a fish became a Christian symbol because the letters of the Greek word for fish, *ichthus* — iota, chi, theta, upsilon, sigma — could be used as an acronym for "Jesus Christ, Son of God, Saviour," in its Greek

ABOVE: Hindu god Vishnu in his avatar incarnation of Matsya (fish).

RIGHT: Marble carving from Monreale Monastry, Sicily.

OPPOSITE ABOVE: Dolphins and fish on a fresco at Knossos, Crete.

OPPOSITE BELOW: A symbol of Christianity.

form. Tales are told that on meeting in ancient times, a person might draw a crescent in the dust and, if the other was Christian, he would draw another, completing the fish sign.

Recently the Christian fish sign has appeared on cars. It has been much parodied, notably with the Darwin fish, which has evolved legs. The Darwin Award given to people who die in a particularly pointless manner, thus not passing on their genes, is a symbolic fish, belly-up. The babelfish from the *Hitchhikers Guide to the Galaxy* series is a symbol for translation, and now a Web site. The Pastafarians have also evolved a fishy sign, with a fish body shape, two eyes on stalks and five "noodly appendages," the symbol of the Flying Spaghetti Monster.

SNAKE

There are hundreds of cosmic, symbolic serpents. There was one in the Garden of Eden. The cobra appeared on Pharaoh's headdress, and Cleopatra

LEFT: Stained glass window in Our Lady of Salette, Sete, France.

OPPOSITE: Harmed mosaic fish, Sousse Museum.

took an asp to her bosom. In India, Nag is the King of Snakes and, during the festival of *Nag Panchami*, snakes are worshipped and offered milk. Indian women often feed milk to snakes, though snakes do not drink it. There are temples to snake deities.

In Hindu belief, Vishnu and the gods and demons used a snake to churn the ocean. Vishnu reclines on a snake, Shesha Naga, who has a thousand heads.

Native Americans and Mesoamericans have many snake

ABOVE: Tlaloc, the Aztec god associated with rain, fertility, and water.

LEFT: Coatlicue, Aztec lady of the serpent skirt.

OPPOSITE LEFT: Hermes and his caduceus or herald staff.

OPPOSITE RIGHT: Teotihuacan plumed serpent.

thunder, and water. The coat of arms of Mexico displays an eagle with a snake in its beak. The Aztec goddess of the earth, life, and death was Coatlicue, who wore a skirt of snakes and had two snakes making up her face. She also wore a necklace of human hearts. She had sharp claws and a thirst for blood. Her husband was Mixcoatl, the cloud serpent.

Snakes appear as heraldic devices. Two snakes coiled around a rod, making a double helix with wings at the top, is the Staff of Hermes. One snake twining on a rod with no wings is the symbol of Asclepius, god of healing. The snake symbolizes wisdom and mystic insight; if it is shedding its skin, it symbolizes death and rebirth.

symbols. Maya, Inca, and Aztec shared a concept of a god who gave man agriculture, language, and knowledge. Some associated the snake with rain,

CHAPTER EIGHT
SYMBOLS FROM HUMANITY

Egypt, China, Mesopotamia, and Mesoamerica are all areas that developed writing systems independently.

The first writing began to emerge in Mesopotamia about 6,000 years ago.

Trading tokens were sealed in clay; then, to save breaking the "envelope," the number was put on the outside. This became obsolete as symbols for numbers and commodities developed.

Some scripts have never been deciphered. The beautiful seals found in the Indus Valley remain a mystery — no one knows which language matches the script.

It helps if a multilingual source can be found, like the Rosetta Stone, found in Egypt in 1799 bearing an inscription in classical Greek, hieroglyphics, and a demotic Egyptian script. It was deciphered in 1822 by Jean-François Champollion. This

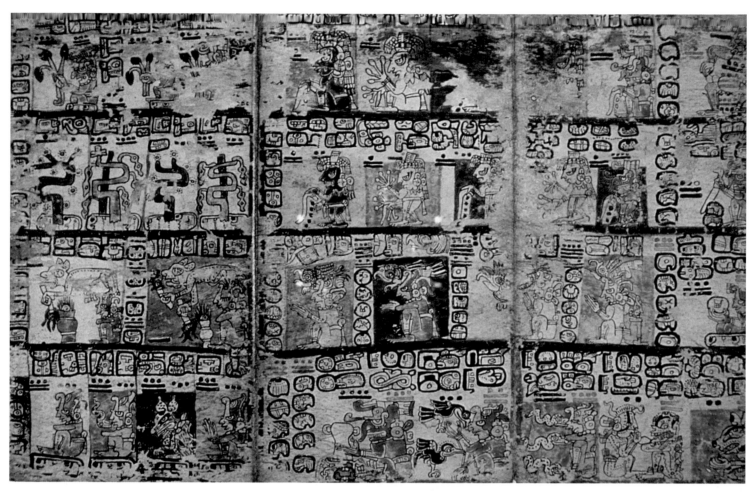

ABOVE: The Madrid Codex, an Aztec scroll.

OPPOSITE: Indus Valley unicorn seal, showing script. Courtesy of UCL Institute of Archaeology.

opened the way to reading hieroglyphs.

Mayan script is like none other: often called hieroglyphics, the system uses both symbols to represent words and syllabaries to make up words. It was seen as a gift from the gods and not for common man.

Much Mayan script was destroyed by the Spanish, but the bishop responsible prevented some of the scripts from being destroyed and thus saved some evidence as to how they might be read.

A major breakthrough though was made by Tatiana Proskouriakoff (1909–86), who showed that certain writings concerned rulers over a 200-year period. Knowing the context, advances have been made in deciphering other inscriptions.

Runes are symbols for Germanic languages, and were held to be of divine origin. Over time, they were replaced by Latin script. Changes in the languages and sounds of the language meant that the runic alphabets themselves changed and developed from area to area and time to time.

Runes were mainly used for short inscriptions — to write a name on a possession, like a comb, or on a memorial stone. This gave rise to the idea that they were used by an elite and were magic signs. The name "rune" means "hidden."

Runes today have mystic uses, being used by occult, hermetic, self-help,

RIGHT: A runestone raised in the memory of Igulger, c.11th century CE, Uppsala, Sweden.

OPPOSITE LEFT: The most ancient Chinese inscriptions are inscribed on this turtle oracle bone dating from 1500–1000 BCE.

OPPOSITE RIGHT: The first human footprint on the moon is a significant image.

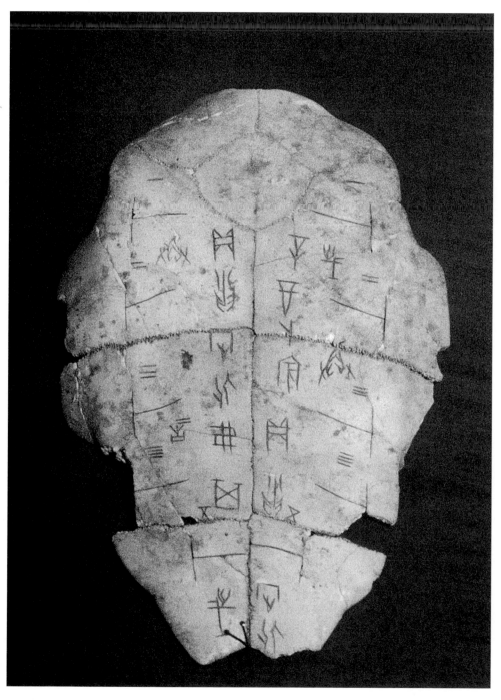

and new age practitioners. Methods of "casting the rune stones" are used for divination.

Some cultures reserve special symbols for specific purposes: Chinese astrologers, for example, use special signs for astrology.

FOOTPRINTS

Carved or natural features, footprints are found all over the world. They are used as symbols in ceremonies; as a focus for devotions; or to recall heroes.

Unintentional symbols are often poignant: the Laetoli footprints, the first footprints of "man" walking upright, and preserved in volcanic mud in Tanzania, represent early links to our common ancestors.

In South Asia, since the second century BCE, footprints have been adorned with symbols of the divine nature of the Buddha — the wheel, floral emblems, and swastikas on the toes.

Not all footprints are ancient: in Thailand, a former prime minister and his wife had one built and crowds celebrate the New Year by pouring water over it.

Hindu deities left many footprints: Vishnu is well represented. A pilgrimage to the footprint of a three-headed Goddess in Kashmir will give devotees strength against evil; prosperity and comfort; and the ability to live virtuous lives.

There are also Islamic and Christian footprints. The footprints of the Prophet are at the Dome of the Rock in Jerusalem. The footprints of

LEFT: The footprint of Buddha at the Temple of the Tooth, Kandy, Sri Lanka.

OPPOSITE LEFT: The footprint of the Prophet Mohammad at the Topkapi Palace, Istanbul.

OPPOSITE RIGHT: The goddess Skadi chose a husband by his feet.

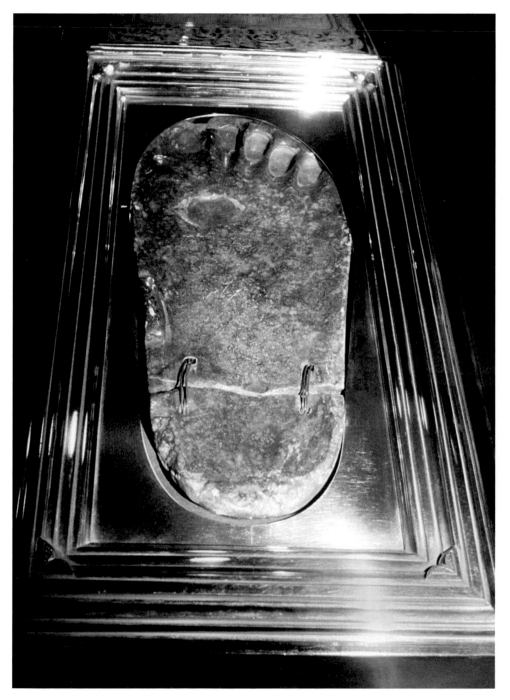

Jesus are believed by some to be found at the Chapel of the Ascension.

Adam's Peak in Sri Lanka is claimed by Buddhists to be a footprint of the Buddha; Hindus revere it as a footprint of Lord Siva; while Muslims and Christians say that it was the print made by Adam as he left the Garden of Eden.

In Scandinavia the footprint is a symbol of the god Njörd. Thor killed

the father of a frost giantess named Skadi; in retribution she was allowed to choose a husband from the gods. The gods were hidden by a curtain and she had to make her choice by looking at their feet. She chose the most beautiful feet, hoping that they belonged to Baldur, god of joy and beauty. But the feet turned out to belong to Njörd, god of the winds, sea, and sky. The footprint was associated with fertility and the Vanir gods.

Handprints

Hands are expressive — the *mudras* of classic Indian dance symbolize the emotions. The meaning of such signs made with the hands varies

ABOVE: An Orthodox blessing, an example of a hand gesture.

RIGHT: Handprints of women who died on their husbands' funeral pyres, Mehergarh Fort, Rajasthan, India.

OPPOSITE: Adam's Peak, in Sri Lanka, is visited by all faiths.

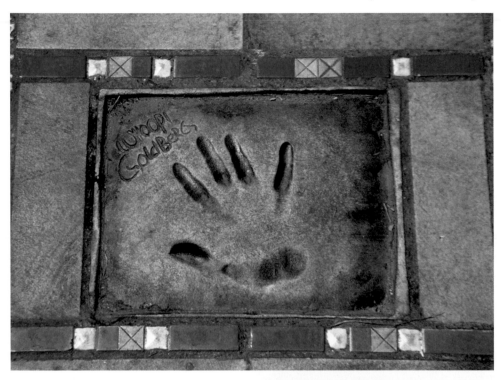

Celtic cultures abound in prints of body parts — mostly feet, but also knees, hands, elbows, heads, and fingers. These date from megalithic times to the early Middle Ages and are plentiful in areas occupied by Picts, Scots, Irish, Welsh, Cornish, and Bretons. There are also prints of miscellaneous animals.

Handprints, footprints, and signatures of celebrities are nowadays collected on "walks of fame." People often keep prints of their babies' hands and feet, or of their cats' paws.

HEART

The heart usually appears as a stylized shape, not actually much like a human

internationally. Just raising one or two fingers has a significant effect in most cultures!

Some of the most disturbing handprints are found in Rajasthan, India, where women burned themselves to death, believing their warrior husbands dead and not wishing to be taken prisoner. There are also the handprints of *satis* — widows who died on their husbands' funeral pyres. The British tried to stop this practice but the last known case was that of an 18-year-old bride in 1987.

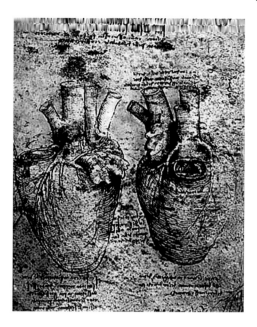

all about love though. Pharaoh in the Old Testament was caused to "harden his heart" by God and to keep the Israelites in captivity. The heart is traditionally more associated with emotion than the brain. Are you ruled by your heart or your head?

The Egyptians weighed the heart and left it in the mummified body, while removing the other organs. It was seen as a symbol of truth.

Maya and Aztec human sacrifices were killed by removing their hearts, in the belief that the gods desired it. The beating heart was a symbol of the sun's power in every aspect of life, and thousands of people needed to be sacrificed to ensure the sun's power. Lifeblood was shed to bring about regeneration.

heart. It symbolizes love and compassion and has mystic significance. Generally, it is related to the ideas of emotion and true love, and is often carved on trees. It's not

ABOVE: Leonardo's anatomical drawing of the human heart.

RIGHT: Canopic jars were used by Egyptians to store significant body parts.

OPPOSITE ABOVE: Whoopi Goldberg obliged with a handprint in Cannes, France.

OPPOSITE LEFT: A stylized heart-shaped balloon.

CLOTHING

The wearing of symbolic clothing is often a source of dissent. France bans all religious symbols and dress in schools, while other countries squirm between enforcing equality in uniforms and political correctness.

Strict dress codes symbolize religiosity. The *Mevlevi* whirling dervishes wear a simple outfit: a white gown representing death, a black cloak representing the grave, and a tall brown hat representing the gravestone. The smiling Quaker on the cereal packet is often seen as a comfortable figure.

Dress can also indicate status. Wearing their regalia, Elizabeth II and the Pope are immediately recognizable, and so is the fool in his motley.

Shakespeare used clothing as symbols: Petruchio's ridiculous wedding outfit in *The Taming of the Shrew* symbolizes his control over Kate. It shows the nature of clothes: the suit isn't the man. Worse still, he controls what Kate wears! In fiction, Victorian heroines wore modest dresses, indicating their modest character. In modern novels, authors create character by reference to designer labels alone. The right logo becomes a convenient shorthand.

LEFT: A headscarf can evoke strong feelings.

BELOW: Mevlevi dervishes wear simple but deeply symbolic attire.

OPPOSITE: Yeoman Warders' tunics are embroidered with flowers symbolizing the countries of the United Kingdom, the royal crown, and the monogram ER — Elizabeth Regina.

The British are noted for ceremonies and ceremonial dress. They joke about "men in tights," but they do

are known for their bright scarlet and gold knee-length tunics, knee breeches, and stockings. Their white ruff was an innovation by Elizabeth I. Seen dancing with Dick Van Dyke in *Mary Poppins*, the working-class Pearly Kings and Queens are another widely recognized group, whose symbolic costumes

exist. Mace Bearers, the Gentleman Usher of the Black Rod, and other officials each have their own uniform, and British uniforms for ceremonial occasions are archaic and magnificent. The Beefeaters at the Tower of London

ABOVE: Teddy boys started young fashion and were resplendent in drape jackets.

RIGHT: A Russian Shaman family wear animal skin clothing that accords with their beliefs.

OPPOSITE: Pearly Kings and Queens.

consist of suits and hats with so many pearl buttons sewn on that the fabric is barely visible. The pearly tradition was founded by Henry Croft (1875–1930), whose statue may be seen in the crypt of St. Martin-in-the-Fields, London. He began wearing pearl-buttoned suits to collect money for charitable purposes.

Pearlies' clothes bear many symbols, some of which relate to family. Others include horseshoes (luck), doves (peace), hearts (charity), anchors (hope), and crosses (faith). Playing cards say "life is a gamble," flowerpots and donkey carts represent costermongers, or apple-sellers. The original Pearlies were barrow boys.

Every subculture has its symbolic dress. Apart from their novels and poems, the Beatniks had their own fashions, which are frequently recycled, with black polo necks, headscarves tied around the neck, and tight black trousers.

In movies from *High Noon* to *Star Wars*, the villain has always worn black, and nowadays each side in futuristic and fantasy films has a highly symbolic uniform, immediately understandable to the audience.

People involved in ceremonies and magic often wear special clothing.

Shamans are found across the world. North American shamanic clothing is decorated with birds and animal protectors, and thus connects to the protective spirit. Mongolian shamans wear inherited clothes that increase their sanctity. These tend to be white dresses and aprons and a sheepskin coat, with many decorative metal items. They wear red hats decorated with horns and sometimes masks. The drumsticks they use have symbolic names such as "flying horses" or "scaly snakes."

GAMES

The original Olympic Games were held in 776 BCE. Each Greek city's games were dedicated to a different god. The prizes were wreaths of leaves.

In 1913 the founder of the modern Olympics, Baron Pierre de Coubertin,

ABOVE RIGHT: The Olympic flag's circles symbolize the five continents.

RIGHT: Celebration of the Olympic Games, a torch relay in Adelaide, Australia.

OPPOSITE: In the movies, villains usually wear black, like Darth Vader in the Star Wars series.

LEFT: Chess is essentially a game of war.

OPPOSITE: All games involve symbols.

saw a Greek artifact that suggested the design of the Olympic flag. It has five circles — blue, yellow, green, black and red — which symbolize the five continents.

The torch, flame, and fire are symbols of the Olympic Games. The flame is kindled on Mount Olympus and travels immense distances to reach the site of the games. Fire has divine connotations, originally having been stolen from Zeus by Prometheus.

The Olympic flame burns in a cauldron, though in modern times the cauldron is often constructed as a striking design feature, and some very spectacular ways of lighting the flame from the torch have been invented. The flame burns throughout the games.

Games are usually a symbolic conflict, played against an opposing individual or team. Superior strategy and guile often win out.

It's impossible to think of games without symbols. Computer game symbols are ubiquitous — who doesn't remember Pac Man, a yellow circle

LEFT: Patolli is a game for gamblers.

OPPOSITE: Go is a popular game in China.

rules of the game are now unknown.

No one knows when dice first appeared, but they are ancient. A Tibetan Buddhist game with dice is played on a board with symbolic squares displaying cosmic geography. Players negotiate paths toward rebirth, liberation and enlightenment.

Chess and Go are very different examples of strategy games, both of great antiquity. Chess is a war game. Archaeologists have found chessmen in various parts of the world. Those found on the Isle of Lewis date from 1150–1170 CE. Modern pieces can be based on battles, politicians, historical events, and stories. Indian chessmen vary slightly from modern sets. They have the vizier (prime minister) elephants, warhorses, and the *rukh* (castle).

Games using the tarot deck have been played in European countries since the 1430s, if not earlier. Most involve four suits, 21 trump cards, and a joker, and points are awarded for

with a wedge removed, who is able to eat his enemies? From *Grand Theft Auto* to *Monopoly*, symbols are used. The entire symbolism of alchemy, magic, grimoires, and spells has been recycled into electronic games.

Board games appeared early in history with the Royal Game of Ur, which dates back to 3000 BCE. The

Egyptian Pharaohs played games, and had boards in their tombs to continue playing in the afterlife. One of the oldest is *Senet*, and rules have been surmised allowing the game to be played today. *Mahen* was played on a board depicting the body of a coiled snake, with pieces shaped as lions and lionesses and some small balls, but the

making tricks. Different European countries also use packs with different symbols for the usual playing cards.

Indian cards, *ganjifa*, are circular. The game is said to have originated in Persia, and was popular at the Moghul court in India. Moghul cards were made of ivory and semi-precious stones. Ganjifa is little played nowadays.

Mesoamerican people enjoyed various games. *Patolli* is an ancient game played with dice and beans on a board with diagonal crossed lines. It is highly competitive, like a war game or a race, and may involve gambling.

Mesoamerican ball games are frequently depicted in art, and different versions of the games have been played over the past 3,000 years in an area stretching from Nicaragua to Arizona. Games are associated with myths about struggles between deities, and they symbolize man's engagement in the cosmic order and the regeneration of life. The game is played in an enclosed long narrow court, and uses a solid, heavy rubber ball — a symbol of the sun, moon, and stars; rings on the walls

LEFT: Court for the Mesoamerican ball game, Honduras.

symbolize sunrise and sunset. Rubber has a symbolic significance, being associated with bodily fluids, and is a symbol of fertility. Rubber balls were often burned before images in shrines. Games were symbolic warfare, often played against prisoners who were then sacrificed. Despite the best efforts of European soccer hooligans, the Mesoamerican ball game makes other ball games seem very tame.

HOMES

The home symbolizes the most important things in life — the family eating and relaxing together. Doors and windows are common metaphors; they can be opened — just as windows in the mind can be opened. They thus require protection from evil. Even keys are an important symbol — a key piece of information often resolves a problem. Keys are also symbols of authority, especially papal authority, with St. Peter's keys to heaven symbolizing the connection between heaven and earth.

Many symbols are used to protect the home. Chinese buildings with their curved roofs, fancy corners, curved paths and red front doors protect against demons that fly only in straight lines. Beams were traditionally crowded

ABOVE: Roof ornaments in England deter or distract witches and keep them at bay.

OPPOSITE: A Chinese teahouse with a curved roof.

with protective ceramic animal figures.

Traditional British thatched roof ornaments, often pheasants and foxes, keep witches away. Alternatively, the witches stop and play with the ornaments and don't do mischief

elsewhere. Modern ornaments include airplanes, fishes, and dragons. Scots grow a protective rowan tree near the door. Many homes nail a horseshoe on the door or lintel to trap the devil in the curve. Horseshoes also bring good luck, but must be placed with the U facing up — otherwise the luck will fall out! Another protector is the sedum, or houseleek. Charlemagne ordered it to be planted on every roof to protect against witches, fire, and lightning.

Chimneys and hearths are a particular danger area. Some cultures have no chimneys and regard smoke as beneficial. A mantelpiece usually has a clock (protective sun), family pictures (protective ancestors) and mirrors, as flashes are feared by demons. Mirrors deflect evil; offer protection, beauty and vitality; and reflect reality. It was common for Welsh miners to have ceramic King Charles spaniels on their mantelpieces. These were usually

OPPOSITE & BELOW: Chimneys and hearths were considered a danger, so traditionally protective items were placed on the mantelpiece, such as Staffordshire dogs.

wedding presents, and both guarded the domestic hearth and also safeguarded

the miner in his dangerous job. Each dog has a padlock and chain, security symbols, around its neck.

Status symbols are found in and on homes the world over. If you walk around the Ringstrasse in Vienna, mansions that were built by the aristocracy bear heraldic and other symbols representing the family and its place in the world. Blocks of apartments for rent are similarly decorated, but with meaningless symbols as the transitory occupants had nothing significant to display.

FABRICS, EMBROIDERY, AND QUILTS
Symbols are frequently embroidered on clothing and household fabrics.

Chinese symbolism is complex. A white crane is the symbol of a high official and it looks toward the sun, showing loyalty to the emperor. Dragons with wisps of flame express their supernatural character and benevolence; certain dragon patterns were reserved for royalty. Butterflies symbolize conjugal happiness, and pink bats, often grouped in fives, symbolize long life, wealth, tranquillity, love of virtue, and a happy death. Birds, flowers, and fruit are also common motifs.

SUPERNATURAL SIGNS, SYMBOLS, AND CODES

The sun, moon, and constellations are among related symbols associated with court dress. The four seasons are shown as a spring peony, summer lotus, autumn chrysanthemum, and prunus flowers (cherries, peaches, and almonds) or poppies for winter. Taoist symbols — flutes, swords, and drums appear — as do Buddhist symbols — canopies, umbrellas, wheels, and knots.

QUILTS

Quilts are often charged with symbolism. At the most basic level, quilts made from discarded family clothing with no attempt at design will at least recall those who wore the clothes and when they wore them.

Quilters sometimes stitch family or national history — American civil war diary quilts, patriotic quilts, or complex symbols such as the Great Seal of the United States. Early African American quilts show designs from African fabric, and some later quilts, mapped the 19th-century Underground Railroad, which assisted escaped slaves fleeing from the USA to Canada.

Some of the most poignant quilts are modern, and contain symbols such as the pink breast-cancer campaign symbol. The AIDS memorial quilt was begun in 1987 in San Francisco as a monument to people who were never given much of a funeral because of fear of the disease. The Names Project Foundation quilt is huge, and each panel is decorated with appropriate symbols to record a loved one.

In eastern India quilts often reflected home life. They still show aspects of traditional village life, but nowadays quilts often lobby for change.

They oppose female infanticide, domestic and political violence, and dowry, and support education for girls. Quilters also campaign to raise AIDS awareness.

PERSONAL SIGNATURES

A personal signature is also proof of identity. Elizabeth I wrote her name clearly, Elizabeth R (for Regina or Queen) ornamented with splendid flourishes. Handwriting experts can interpret much, even from a scrawl.

Among the earliest recognized signatures is the cartouche, an Egyptian or Mayan oblong shape with

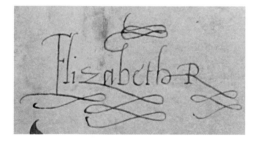

ABOVE: Elizabeth I's signature.

OPPOSITE: This Chinese embroidered dragon is a symbol of benevolence.

RIGHT: The 15,000 panels of the AIDS memorial quilt laid out on The Mall in Washington, D.C.

a royal name.

The *tughra* is a seal or signature of an Ottoman Sultan. It is made up of complex calligraphy. The *tughra* of Suleiman the Magnificent is the most beautiful of all.

Every line and element of the *tughra* is symbolic, and shows the power and influence of the Sultan and the lands he ruled.

Sufis also have *tughras*, the most famous being the winged heart, the seal of the Sufis of the West. Founded by Hazrat Inayat Khan, the *tughras* of Sufi organizations are emblematic calligraphy, forming the name of the founder of their tradition.

In India, Hindu stonecutters often

BELOW: Tughra of Sultan Mahmoud II at the Topkapi Palace, Istanbul

OPPOSITE LEFT: Chi and rho are the first two letters of the word "Christ."

OPPOSITE RIGHT: Seal of Edward III of England, 1364.

groups. The chi-rho combination represents the first two letters of "Christ," and was used on Constantine's battle standards. The abbreviation "X" comes from it.

Great seals, rings, and signets show power and authority, and make an impression in more ways than one. Used from earliest times in the India Valley and Mesopotamia, they allowed authority to be delegated, as the signet ring or seal could be used by different people.

found Islamic calligraphy difficult, but there are still many *tughras* on buildings. These are unintelligible to most people because of the particularly artistic use of letters. In Bengal, votaries poured milk and oil over the inscriptions, taking them as powerful amulets, and sick people tried to catch the liquid as a cure. The holy words carry the power of blessing, even if they are not understood.

In monograms and initials, several letters may be combined into one symbol and used by individuals or

209

CHAPTER NINE
GEOGLYPHS, PYRAMIDS, SPIRALS, MAZES, CIRCLES & THE WHEEL

The most famous drawings on the earth's surface are the Nazca lines, created in Peru between 200 BCE and 700 CE. Best viewed from the air, they represent hummingbirds, llamas, lizards, spiders, fish, and monkeys. They were laid out, presumably with considerable planning, with a system of stakes and lines. It is not known why the figures were created, but academics reject the notion of landing strips for spacecraft.

Australian aboriginal people also produced geometrical stone arrangements.

Some impressive stone arrangements are found in Britain — the

RIGHT: A hummingbird motif from Nazca.

OPPOSITE: Climbing through the center of the Men-an-Tol cures fertility problems and rheumatism.

many stone circles, the best known being Stonehenge and Avebury. British stone monuments are not only set in circles. A very odd one is the Men-an-Tol in Cornwall, which has two straight stones and one holed one, such that it looks like the number 101. Various ideas abound: perhaps fertility can be assured or rheumatism cured by

climbing through the hole in the "o." Carnac in Brittany has a huge formation with approximately 3,000 menhirs (large stones) set in lines.

In the United States, mounds were made by the Hopewell Indians who produced the Death Mask Mound at Chillicothe, Ohio. Another earthwork is the Ohio Serpent Mound, representing

an enormous snake ingesting an egg. If stretched out it would be about 1,250 feet (381 m) long. In Southern California, an image dating from *c*.90 CE, is said to be connected with tribal myths. It was constructed by ancestors of the Mohawks.

HILL FIGURES

Hill figures are found mostly in the south of England on chalk hills called "downs." They are made by taking away the grass and topsoil to reveal the white chalk underneath. No one knows when or why people began to carve such figures on the landscape. The oldest is the white horse at Uffington, and is thought to date from the early Iron Age. Other figures are far more recent. Most figures are solid, but a few, like the Cerne Abbas giant and the Long Man of Wilmington, are outlines. Cerne Abbas is the largest such figure. Grass and weeds continually invade the figures, covering the chalk. It is said that on May Day young couples used to climb the "downs" and clean the figures before rolling (in couples) down the hill. Puritans wanted an end to this unseemly behavior, and since then maintenance has become more difficult.

ABOVE: Hopewell Indians produced many earthworks, including the Death Mask Mound at Chillicothe, Ohio.

OPPOSITE: The Long Man of Wilmington is a famous geoglyph (or hill figure) that can be seen from the sky over South Downs, Sussex, in England.

Hill figures are not always treated with great solemnity. The *Big Brother* (television show) logo, an eye, was painted with water-soluble paint near the ancient Uffington horse.

A beautiful and recent addition to the chalk figures of England is the

horse, and it is the first thing seen on entering the UK. It was initially laid out in canvas, and then slabs were laid by the Gurkhas from nearby barracks. The project was directed by short-range radio, which must have been easier than the earlier method of using chains of people to pass messages. A time capsule was buried at the site, and the horse's eye is described as being sited on a "powerful earth energy site."

PYRAMIDS

The Chinese, Egyptians, Mesopotamians, Europeans, and

horse at Folkestone, Kent, near the Channel Tunnel entrance. It seems fitting to have marked the millennium with a revival of an ancient custom. The design, while recalling the most ancient design at Uffington, is pleasing and modern. It is a joyful, galloping

RIGHT: The pyramid of Cheops and the Sphnyx, Egypt.

ABOVE: The Millennium Horse at Folkestone, Kent.

OPPOSITE: The oldest of them all, the White Horse at Uffington, England.

GEOGLYPHS, PYRAMIDS, SPIRALS, MAZES, CIRCLES & THE WHEEL

Mesoamericans all built pyramids. A pyramid is the easiest, most stable large structure that can be built. The pyramid symbolizes unity, harmony, mountains, and ascension.

Pyramid-shaped gravestones appealed to many Freemasons in the Southern States of America, ensuring no Yankees would sit on them!

Urban myth and conspiracy theorists love pyramids, claiming for example that the glass pyramid entrance to the Louvre Museum, built in 1989, is made from 666 pieces of glass: actually, 603 rhombus-shaped pieces and 70 triangles were used. 666 is no longer the powerful symbol it once was, as scholars suggest "the number of the beast" is actually 616 or 665.

BELOW: The pyramid-shaped Ras Salmiya Mosque in Kuwait is a fine example of modern architecture, and certainly an unusual design for a mosque.

OPPOSITE: Pyramid at the entrance to the Louvre Museum, Paris, France.

RIGHT: A double spiral at Newgrange, Meath, Ireland.

BELOW: A baby and a skull surrounded by an ouroboros: "Finis Aborigine Pedet" means "look for the end in the beginning."

BELOW RIGHT: Mary Queen of Scots.

OPPOSITE: The maze at Hampton Court.

SPIRALS AND MAZES

Spirals are ancient symbols found on rock faces and stones, but their meaning is unknown. Spirals are associated with water and power, and water is itself a symbol for purification. Celtic spirals sometimes come in threes; no one knows what the ancient ones symbolize, but modern ones usually represent the Trinity, or various triple aspects of Wicca. Spirals appear on carpets and tapestries, and are believed to have powers of protection.

A maze is a puzzle, either with a single route or branching routes to the center. Some are for amusement only; others symbolize a path from birth (the entrance) to god (the center). They are a symbolic pilgrimage and an aid to meditation. A maze is a dead end with a useful thread.

The maze related closely to music and dance and is reflected in the

medieval palindromic round *En ma vie est mon commencement et mon commencement ma fin* (My end is my beginning and my beginning my end), a saying that was adopted as a motto by Mary Queen of Scots, who embroidered it, along with anagrams and symbols such as the phoenix, to pass the time in prison.

Mazes were often planted for aristocrats. The most famous, at Hampton Court near London, was planted between 1689 and 1695 for William of Orange. In the 1970s maze designers began to fashion mazes from plants, turf, maize, and many other materials.

The words "labyrinth" and "maze" are often used interchangeably, but in fact a labyrinth is a unicursal path, not a puzzle where you can often get lost, though clearly the original labyrinth at Knossos, where the Minotaur was kept, was a complex one.

CIRCLES

Circles are a potent symbol of cosmic unity, harmony, balance, equilibrium, the hidden center, and the timeless dimensionless point of encompassing space.

Patterns and arabesques used in Muslim buildings are not mere decorative motifs; they show the mathematical order and harmony in the cosmos. Concentric circles and many circular patterns have no beginning and no end.

The domes of huge Turkish mosques are capped by massive cupolas, breathtaking and seemingly

LEFT: An ancient labyrinth at Tintagel, Cornwall, England.

RIGHT: The Great Dome of Sinan's Sulemaniye Mosque in Istanbul channels heavenly peace down on to worshippers.

221

unsupported, symbolizing peace and infinity.

The Parliament of India in New Delhi, *Sansad Bhavan*, was built by the British in 1912–13. The roof is supported by 157 granite columns. The circle is appropriate because the spinning wheel was promoted by Mahatma Gandhi. The Indian flag also shows a symbolic wheel.

The circle contains yin and yang, heaven and earth, the duality being a major concept in Chinese medicine and philosophy. Yin and yang symbolize opposing yet complementary forces in the universe. The circle is divided by a curved line, the black side symbolizing darkness and the female, and the white symbolizing lightness and the male. Each half has a dot of the opposing

color, showing that they are balanced and interdependent, a perfect equilibrium between opposing principles.

Yin and yang come from Taoist belief, based on the unity of man and the cosmos and the complementary nature of the energy symbolized in yin

ABOVE: The yin and yang symbol.

LEFT: The dome of the monastery of the Holy Cross in Samos — blessings and power descend from Christ Pantocrator.

OPPOSITE ABOVE: The Indian Parliament building in New Delhi has a circular design.

OPPOSITE BELOW: Head of Fortuna, Corinth, Greece.

and yang. The I Ching, or *Chinese Book of Changes*, communicates through 64 hexagrams. Eight trigrams are combined, symbolizing many things — family members, animals, elements, seasons and weather, and qualities like strength, docility, dependence, and danger.

THE WHEEL

The wheel was originally that of Fortuna, the Roman goddess of Fate, "she who revolves the year." The sixth-century scholar Boethius observed that random turns of the wheel are inevitable, part of god's plan, so man should not resist or try to change things.

The wheel was an important sign in Medieval imagination. Rose windows show the cycle of fortune in stained glass — "I shall reign"; "I reign"; "I have reigned"; and "I have no kingdom."

Both Chaucer and Shakespeare mention the wheel. Many of Chaucer's characters suffer wild turns of fate as the wheel turns. Shakespeare's *Hamlet* speaks of the "the slings and arrows of outrageous fortune," and wants "to break all the spokes and fellies from her

223

LEFT: *The huge rose window of St. Malo Cathedral, France.*

OPPOSITE: *The wheel of life between two deer on the roof of the Monastery of Deprung, Tibet.*

wheel," referring to the strumpet Fortune. *Henry V* has a reference to "Fortune's furious, fickle wheel." *King Lear* contains the line "Fortune, goodnight, smile once more; and turn thy wheel!"

Nowadays, the wheel of fortune is associated with games and television shows, misfortune often said to be due to "having a stick in their spokes."

The flag of India shows Ashoka's chakra, a wheel with 24 spokes. Ashoka (304–232 BCE) was a great emperor. The wheel symbolizes the cycle of time and the four ages — the Golden Age; the Silver Age; the Copper Age; and the Iron Age. Each age deteriorates, and we have the misfortune to inhabit the Iron Age, the worst age of all.

The twenty-four spokes symbolize love, courage, patience, peacefulness, kindness, goodness, faithfulness,

GEOGLYPHS, PYRAMIDS, SPIRALS, MAZES, CIRCLES & THE WHEEL

gentleness, self-control, selflessness, truthfulness, righteousness, justice, mercy, graciousness, humility, empathy, sympathy, godly knowledge, morality, fear of god, and trust in the goodness of god.

The wheel is also a Buddhist symbol. The spokes represent the Buddha's teaching, the eightfold path, and the circle shows the cycle of samsara or rebirth.

The spinning wheel was associated with Mahatma Gandhi, and was displayed on the flag of the Indian independence movement.

CHAPTER TEN
LIGHT, MUSIC & DANCE

LIGHT

Why does a light bulb symbolize a good idea? Cartoonists often use this symbolization.

Light is a symbol of truth, purification, and lighting the darkness, expelling evil and ignorance.

There is a saying that it is better to light a candle than to curse the darkness. This is either an ancient Chinese proverb, or a quotation from Adlai Stevenson about Eleanor Roosevelt. "She would rather light candles than curse the darkness, and her glow has warmed the world."

Light is a religious symbol: the Star of Bethlehem led the Magi on their journey, and the child they visited came to be called "the light of the world." "Lighten our darkness we beseech thee, O Lord, and by thy great mercy defend us from all the perils and dangers of this night" is an often quoted prayer.

"Bell, book, and candle" is a ceremony in which the candle is

226

LEFT: A shepherd sees the Star of Bethlehem; painted in the Chapelle de Penitents Blanc at Les Baux, France.

OPPOSITE: The Statue of Liberty's torch symbolizes enlightenment.

extinguished and the book closed. When the bell is rung, one who has committed some terrible sin is excommunicated from the Roman Catholic Church. Shakespeare said, "Bell, book and candle shall not drive me back, when gold and silver becks me to come on."

The candle is used as a symbol of teaching in Buddhism and Sikhism. A candle that is used to light a second candle passes on a message.

The Christians were not the first to use the halo. The ancient Egyptians drew haloes on bulls and the ancient Greeks and Romans on deities. Helios, the sun god, has a full halo to show his light. Artists in the west did not always use halos — Leonardo da Vinci's *Last Supper* shows no halos, though an arch symbolizes one.

Halos are common in Indian art. Buddha, Hindu deities, Sikh gurus, and Moghul emperors often had large, solar halos. The sun and moon halos

supported by angels symbolize some Moghul ideas about kingship.

The seven-branched candlestick is one of the oldest and best-known Jewish symbols.

At Hanukkah, Jewish families light candles on a nine-branched *menorah*. A Hanukiyah commemorates the Maccabees' victory and the miracle that oil continued to burn in their temple for eight days. It suggests freedom and hope. The more usual seven-branched *menorah* has a long history and is a symbol of the nation. The *menorah* resembles a tree that links to spiritual

OPPOSITE LEFT: Bell, book, and candle.

OPPOSITE RIGHT: In Christian art, a halo shows a pure heart, holiness, and the light of grace from God. Christ shown with sacred heart and halo at Santa Agata, Catania, Sicily.

RIGHT: Menorah above the door of a Bordeaux synagogue, France.

BELOW: Buddha with halo, meditating under a Bodhi tree.

regeneration.

During India's festival of lights, *Diwali*, people clean their homes and place "divas" — small earthenware lamps with a wick and oil — along walls and around doors to attract Lakshmi, the goddess of wealth, to their home. It is also a time for gambling. Various other events are celebrated at *Diwali*, including the story of Rama and Sita coming home to their kingdom. Essentially, it is a festival celebrating light triumphing over darkness.

Today, the bright lights of the city signify hope and adventure. The saying, "Will the last to leave turn off the lights?" means that things can't get worse.

and song to capture celestial benefit. Tones were aural symbols, as important as drawn ones.

Robert Fludd, Agrippa, Johannes Kepler, and Athanasius Kirchner thought that universal harmony was viable as a means to understand the universe.

Schopenhauer thought music the most superior art and said that it represented the process of the will at work — cosmic manifestation. Wagner

MUSIC IS THE MOST SYMBOLIC OF THE ARTS

From ancient times, men have believed that, in their geocentric universe, the stars and planets are on spheres that circle the earth, creating perfect harmony as they rotate. Even Copernicus did not discard the spheres; he just rearranged them. It was a commonplace idea, and in Shakespeare's *As You Like It* the duke jokes that "a discord in the spheres" was more likely than Jacques developing musical talent.

It was believed that the soul ascended through the spheres, hearing the music as it traveled. The soul could be dead or that of a person in a trance or dream, rising to the harmony of the invisible world. Souls also descend, taking on the qualities of the planets they encounter. This influences the qualities summarized in a natal horoscope.

Celestial harmony and the use of tone and words in magic were part of Renaissance man's belief. Marsilio Ficino wrote about the power of words

accepted his views, and having something of a Buddhist tendency, came to express views that were similar to those of the Theosophists. Karlheinz Stockhausen

ABOVE: Ponte de Lima Museum in Portugal has an example of early sheet music.

OPPOSITE RIGHT: A bas-relief slab with cuneiform inscription, Nimrud, Iraq.

OPPOSITE LEFT: Angels play their lutes, Church of Maria Maggiore, Rome.

said, "Music should above all be a means to keep awake the connection of the soul with the other side."

MUSICAL NOTATION

Finding symbols for musical notes proved difficult. The earliest attempt is believed to be on a cuneiform tablet found at Nippur, dating from 2000 BCE.

The ancient Greeks had their own system of notation. In about 200 BCE, the Indian scholar Pingala created a system of symbols to indicate long and short syllables in Sanskrit poetry. The Chinese and Japanese and many other groups developed their own methods.

In the eighth century, monks developed a simple system for plainsong. Guido d'Arezzo (995–1050) is credited with the development of a four-line stave and notes. His name is associated with the Guidonian hand, a symbolic memory system in which parts of the hand and fingers represent specific musical notes. Plainsong was the usual form of ecclesiastical music and required only a simple form of writing. From the time of the laying of the foundation stone of Notre Dame de Paris in 1163, the cathedral became a center of musical excellence and development. During a century of musical change, the master Léonin introduced duets, followed by Pérotin, who introduced polyphony — music with four independent voices. These forms required more complex notation. Written with notes on a stave, the scores could be read by anyone and the music could be sung anywhere. A collection of scores, called the *Magnus Liber Organi*, spread across Europe.

Modern musical notation is often credited to Jean Jacques Rousseau in 1742, though at the time his system failed to impress.

LEFT: The lovers Chopin and Georges Sand retreated to a cell at the Real Cartoixa Monastery in Mallorca, Spain, but the wet and miserable winter spent there in 1838–39 ended the affair. This manuscript is of music composed during their stay.

OPPOSITE LEFT: Marching in the Fourth of July parade in Boston, Massachusetts.

OPPOSITE RIGHT: Preparation for a Kathakali performance takes time.

BELOW: The Lord of the Dance is a symbol of India and her culture.

MODERN MUSIC

There are songs for every occasion: work, weddings, funerals, religious occasions, and hunting songs. A minor chord sounds sad and a major chord happy. Everyone recognizes the blues. The Radetsky March is performed at the New Year's Concert in Vienna and a John Philip Sousa march symbolizes America. *Nkosi Sikelele iAfrica* requires no explanation, even though the words are in five languages.

When Tony Bennett first saw MTV, he observed, "In three minutes, they were symbolizing a whole story…You can tell a whole story in 32 bars instead of a 1900-page book."

DANCE

Dance is a dialogue between the dancers and an audience using symbols that include gestures, mimes, masks, costumes and props, and makeup or body painting.

In India, *mudras* (symbolic gestures) are vital. The hands and fingers convey complex conversations, invoking knowledge, dispelling fear, expressing welcome, charity and compassion, and many other emotions.

The flames circling the figure of Siva Nataraja represent the universe. The deity creates and destroys; this is symbolized in the figure. Four arms represent the compass points and the omnipresence of god. The upper right hand holds a drum, which makes the sound of creation, and the left hand holds the flames of destruction. The lower right hand shows the *mudra* giving protection, and the left hand points to the right foot, symbolizing release from the circle of transmigration of the soul. The dwarf under his feet is Purusha, symbolizing man's ignorance.

Kathakali is a complex dance form, famous for its extraordinary costumes and the modeling and painting of faces. *Mudras* and facial expressions tell the story, displaying ridicule, pathos, wrath, and other emotions.

The dances of Native North Americans symbolize important aspects of their lives. Various versions of the Sun Dance are performed, demonstrating relations with nature, and with emphasis on symbolic animals, especially the eagle and the buffalo.

A dance of the Algonquin people was recorded in a drawing from the time when Sir Walter Raleigh arrived in America. The dancers moved around ancestral posts carrying plants, which symbolized the desired harvest.

233

English maypole dances were performed to promote fertility. They were feared by the ruling classes who worried that carnal desires would be encouraged and that magic might be involved. The Puritans were terrified of the devil and eschewed anything that might attract his attention, so they banned maypoles and Christmas celebrations.

RIGHT: Ballet tells stories through symbolism. Darcy Bussell and Rupert Pennefather of the Royal Ballet.

OPPOSITE: Dancers at the Arizona Navaho Fair.

235

CHAPTER ELEVEN
STARS & THE ZODIAC

Stars are a universal symbol, often appearing on flags and military insignia. In heraldry they denoted knightly rank.

Red stars were commonly used by communist regimes. With a crescent moon, they are a symbol of Islam and appear on the flags of Turkey and Pakistan.

The six-pointed star of two interlaced triangles is the Star of David, an ancient Jewish symbol, nowadays associated with the flag of Israel and with Zionism. It is used as jewelry and on pottery.

The Moghul Emperor Humayun has a six-pointed star on his tomb in Delhi. This is considered a Hindu symbol, a union of Lord Siva and Shakti, the powerful goddess.

Humayun spent much time in Persia

RIGHT: A red star adorns the Spasskaya Tower in Moscow.

OPPOSITE ABOVE LEFT: Turkish flag in flowers at the Blue Mosque, Istanbul.

OPPOSITE BELOW LEFT: A Star of David on a plate.

OPPOSITE ABOVE RIGHT: The pentacle is used in symbolic jewelry.

and brought much art and culture back with him, so it may have been imported to India. The star is used in *mandalas*.

A five-pointed star is the symbol of the Druze, a religious community who live in Israel and neighboring countries. They are believed to be an offshoot of Ismaili Islam, Gnosticism, and Neo-Platonism. The star has five colors: green, representing universal mind; red, universal soul; yellow, truth and the word; blue, the antagonist and the cause; and white, the protagonist and the effect.

The five-pointed star is associated with many goddesses. Ceres, the goddess of agriculture and harvests is associated with the apple, which when cut across, displays a five-pointed star at the core.

Unicursal stars are associated with mysticism and magic. The words "pentagram"and "pentacle" are often used without distinction. However, the pentacle is a five-pointed star in a circle, frequently used as jewelry, and the pentagram is a drawn figure for ritual use. When upright, with one point at the top, it is an ancient sign used by Jews and Christians, and

latterly by magicians and Wicca. It can also be inverted with the head of Baphomet superimposed — to appeal to 20th-century Satanists.

Most symbolic stars have five or six points, but more are possible.

THE ZODIAC

The zodiac relates to the belief that the cosmos affects life on earth. The word "zodiac" comes from the Greek, *zodia,* meaning animals. The patterns of the stars do not closely resemble the animals they represent.

The Babylonians were aware of seven "wandering stars" — the planets — which made their circuit aross the sky. The Egyptians painted zodiacs with constellations, working from their ten-day week. The Greeks defined relationships between the wandering stars and constellations. The Roman zodiac had gods and godesses asigned to the signs. Ceres, the corn goddess, was attached to Virgo and watery Neptune to Pisces. In the *Satyricon*, the Roman writer Petronius made fun of a banquet given by a man with more money than sense, where the food entered from the signs of the zodiac.

Early Christianity was opposed to any idea that fate was determined by stars because man is responsible for his actions. The symbols marked the time for various human activities, such as seed planting and harvesting. The zodiac illustrated the year's work and appeared in art in the churches.

The position of signs in the sky changed over time, because the wobble in the earth's axis moved the equinoxes,

OPPOSITE: Stars appear on many flags. The stars, arranged in a quincunx pattern, symbolize the states of the USA.

RIGHT: An armillary sphere is a spherical astrolabe; the rings represent the principle circles of heaven. They were invented in the Middle Ages in the Islamic world. This example is from 18th-century France.

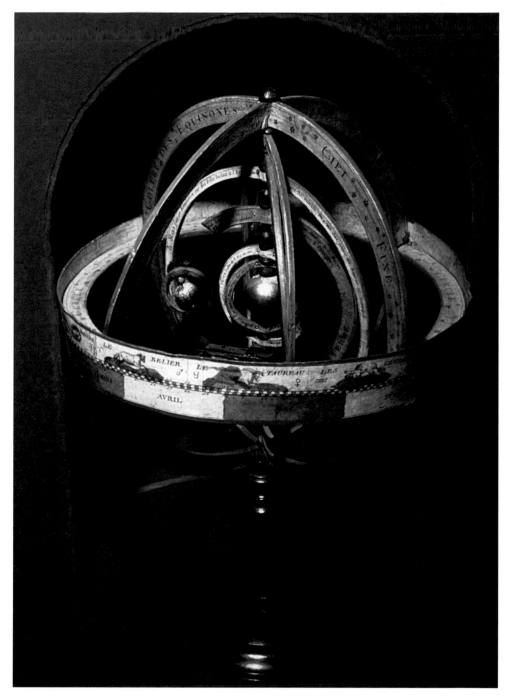

equinoxes. They were once Aries, Cancer, Capricorn, and Libra. Hence the symbol "Y," the Ram's horns, is a symbol for the vernal equinox.

The planets were important to Renaissance scholars. The sun was associated with justice, power, luck, and creativity. The moon governed emotional responses, feelings, and needs. It is related to motherhood, dreams, memories, and the sea. Mercury was a star of communication, associated with curiosity, inventive minds, trade, and business. Mars was a difficult star, being associated with war and brutality, but it could also bring energy, courage, and success. Venus was friendly and femimine, and so was attached to beauty, love, the home, pleasure, family, harmony, and renewal. Jupiter was happy and optimistic and brought money, travel, and generosity, but also a strong moral sense. Saturn was slow and far away, and was associated with depression, learning, and old age.

The planets reflect man's life on earth. Shakespeare writes of the seven ages of man: the mewling infant is associated with the moon and growth; the whining schoolboy with Mercury and education; the lover with Venus and

solstices, and attached signs westward. In the classical era, the sun passed into Aries, marking the first day of spring, and arrived at Virgo with the wheat sheaf as autumn came. There were wet, winter days thoughout Capricorn (water goat), Aquarius (water carrier), and the fishy Pisces. The change in the positions of the signs also changed the position of the

ABOVE LEFT: Aries symbolizes spring.

BELOW LEFT: Virgo is a sign that autumn is here.

BELOW: Watery fishes swimming about symbolize Pisces.

OPPOSITE: Signs of the zodiac on an astronomical clock on the Campanile, Duomo Messina, Italy.

emotion; the soldier with Mars and ambition; the citizen with the sun and virility; the judge with Jupiter and reflection. The old man is associated

with Saturn and resignation.

Some expressions from astrology are in daily use: moonstruck, lunatic, jovial, saturnine, mercurial, and born under a wandering star.

RENAISSANCE ASTROLOGY

In Renaissance times, a system existed using a concentric wheel as an aide to memory. The inner wheel showed the zodiac, planets, sun, and moon, and the outer wheel portrayed man, arts, and sciences. Some believed that by manipulating the wheels, stellar influences on the earth could be manipulated and events could be

influenced.

The signs were also used in medicine. Each body part related to a sign, and birth governed parts of the body. Headaches were related to Aries and bad food to Pisces; the rest of the zodiac was arranged down the torso. Signs were also related to the four elements, which were seen as an important factor in disease. Treatment was based on using materials governed by the same sign.

INDIAN ASTROLOGY

India is the birthplace of Vedic astrology. Charts are prepared when babies are born, and the charts of both partners should be compatible when marriage is considered. Astrologers are consulted about difficult dilemmas and

OPPOSITE RIGHT: Astrology was so important in India in 1928 that the ruler of Jaipur had an observatory constructed: the Jantra Mantra.

OPPOSITE LEFT: The twelve animals of the Chinese zodiac chart.

BELOW: Beautifully carved ivory animals from the Chinese zodiac.

auspicious dates for new enterprises. Bollywood film employees start work on a mahurath or auspicious time. In Indian astrology, the signs align to the stars in the sky.

CHINESE ASTROLOGY

The only symbol (almost) shared by the Chinese with western astrology is the ram; the Chinese have a sheep. Chinese astrology does not relate to constellations but to a system of double hours in the day and month. Each sign governs a different year.

The Chinese system revolves on a sixty-year cycle of five elements and a twelve-year cycle of animal signs that relate to observations of the orbit of Jupiter. As in India, fate and destiny can be calculated from the birth chart, which combines the Chinese system of geomancy known as *feng shui*.

CHAPTER TWELVE
READING SYMBOLS

OF CRUELTY

The villagers of Boule-d'Amont, a village in the Languedoc-Rousillion region of France, take symbolism to an unusual level. The Cross of Cruelty itemizes the sufferings of Christ. It shows a simple but deep devotion.

The horizontal bar (from left to right) shows:

A hammer and a nail, which were used for the crucifixion.

A scourge, a whip, which was used for the scourging.

A lantern, evoking memories of the night Christ was arrested.

A chalice that symbolizes the torment and pain inflicted on him.

A hand — Pontius Pilate gave his judgment having washed his hands.

A pitcher and washbasin recall Pontius Pilate's actions.

Some pincers, used to take the crucified down from the cross.

The vertical bar from the top down shows:

A cockerel, the crowing of which announced the denial of Christ by St. Peter.

The legend INRI, meaning Jesus Nazareus Rex Judaeorum — Jesus of Nazareth, King of the Jews.

The crown of thorns that was placed on Christ's head.

The impression of Christ's face on St. Veronica's handkerchief.

Below the bar:

A purse, bringing to mind the pieces of silver offered to Judas Iscariot, for his betrayal.

A red tunic, a symbol of the royalty of Jesus.

The sword, which cut off the ear of one of the soldiers who came to arrest Christ.

A palm frond, as these were used to welcome Christ to Jerusalem.

The bole of a tree, to which Christ was tied at the time he was scourged.

Some dice for gaming. The centurions drew lots to see who should get the red tunic.

Some coins — representing the money Judas was given.

The ladder used to bring Christ down from the cross.

Finally, on the left, a sponge attached to a pole was used to offer vinegar to drink during the crucifixion.

On the right, the spear used to pierce Christ's side — the Spear of Longinus.

ELIZABETH II

The Crown Jewels are kept in the Tower of London. If they are removed, a small sign replaces them: "In use."

The crowns include St. Edward's

RIGHT: The Cross of Cruelty, Boule-d'Amont, Langusdoc-Rousillion, France.

crown, which was used for the coronation of Elizabeth II. It is used only for the coronation, and on other occasions another state or imperial crown is worn. Crowns symbolize monarchy, guardianship, and power.

The two scepters are the scepter with the cross, symbolizing temporal powers of the sovereign, and the scepter with the dove, the rod of equity and mercy, symbolizing the spiritual role of the monarch.

The orb is a sphere, dating from 1661. It has a band of jewels and a band on the upper hemisphere. The cross is the sign of the "Defender of the Faith," a title earned by Henry VIII, and of sovereignty.

Five swords are used in the coronation. The jeweled Sword of Offering bears the floral emblems of the UK and symbolizes royal authority. The Sword of State is carried before the monarch at the coronation and at the opening of Parliament.

The other swords represent spiritual justice, temporal justice, and mercy — the latter has a blunt tip.

The ring is a sign of royal dignity and of marriage to the nation. Armills are bracelets, symbolizing sincerity and wisdom. New armills were given by the

ST. EDWARD'S CROWN

THE HEAD OF THE KING'S ROYAL SCEPTRE

THE AMPULLA

THE SPOON

THE KING'S ORB

commonwealth countries to Queen Elizabeth II.

The ampulla is a golden eagle flask of anointing oil. It comes with an anointing spoon that survived Oliver Cromwell's destruction. Anointing is an Old Testament tradition: "He has anointed my head with oil, and my cup runneth over." "The spirit of the Lord is with me, because he anointed me." Anointing expresses consecration and the strength needed to exercise authority.

The monarch is also given spurs, representing knighthood and chivalry.

Other countries have Crown Jewels, though the British seem to make most use of them. The Crown Jewels of Hungary are a symbol of national prestige and power, and have been moved from the National Museum to the Parliament Building. The jewels include an orb, scepter, mantle, and St. Stephen's crown. The latter has pendants dangling on chains, four on each side and one at the back, and a crooked cross on top. The cross was damaged sometime in the 16th–17th

LEFT: Some of the British crown jewels.

OPPOSITE: Ganesh.

centuries.

Another ~~symbol that has been changed~~ is the three-tiered Papal Tiara. A symbol of the papacy, it is believed to have Byzantine and Persian origins.

John Paul I and his successor John Paul II dispensed with the tiara, and it does not appear on the arms of Benedict XVI. The other papal symbol is St. Peter's crossed keys.

GANESH

Ganesh is a joyful deity and associated with good fortune. He is printed on wedding invitations. At new year, the merchants and businessmen gather and open new account books, appropriately decorated with symbols of Ganesh. He is associated with wisdom and intelligence, success, prosperity, and protection. He is a symbol of abundance and knowledge, the bringer of joy, and the remover of obstacles.

His large elephant head symbolizes wisdom and the soul: his human body symbolizes earthly existence and plenty.

He has one tusk; the other is broken, symbolizing sacrifice.

Ganesh usually has four arms, but there can be just two, or as many as twelve or fourteen. Numerous arms symbolize power, as many hands can

carry well over fifty symbols. Some hands form *mudras* — symbolic gestures, by which he grants boons or dismisses fears. Two hands invariably hold a noose and an *ankus*, an elephant goad, to steer humans along on the right path. The noose is to snare difficulties and symbolizes worldly attachments and desires, which can lead to the noose. Sometimes Ganesh has an axe to cut through problems and destroy evil. He may have a rosary, symbolizing continual pursuit of knowledge.

Ganesh is associated with the Indian sweet *laddoo*, which shows the sweetness of the soul.

With his large elephant ears, he can hear us. The snake around his waist symbolizes energy. The sacred thread from his left shoulder shows that he is twice born, meaning that he is a member of the first three *varnas* of the Hindu *dharma*, the higher ranks of society.

Bright red is associated with Ganesh, and representations of him are sometimes coated with vermilion paste. Silver foil may also be placed on him as an offering.

Although the West may find Hindu art confusing, there is a precise iconometry involved. The geometry of image-making is a serious subject, and only a correctly made image is suitable as a residence for a deity. If the image does not conform to exact rules and measurements, it is useless.

ISLAMIC TOMB

The Dome of the Rock in Jerusalem symbolizes the universe. The Dome is the axis, the place where heaven and earth meet. Tombs of saints and Sufis are modeled upon the Dome.

At ground level, the plinth is square, symbolizing the fixed, earthly realm — symmetry, equilibrium, and stability.

Above the plinth is an octagonal shape. The number eight is seen as a primary step in the mathematical progression from the square to the circle of the dome, which symbolizes heavenly perfection. The transformation from square to dome is a metaphor for the transformation of the soul.

Muslims see domes as symbolizing how the grace of heaven falls upon us, and this can be seen at its most impressive in buildings such as the Sulemaniya and the Blue Mosque designed by Sinan (1489–1588), in Istanbul. The immensity of the apparently unsupported domes and their exquisite decoration is breathtaking.

The occupants of tombs have completed their journey to heaven, and because they have shared something of the Prophet's *barakah* — his spiritual wisdom and blessing — and are linked through his esoteric teaching, shrines share a metaphysical link as well as a symbolic one.

Decoration depends on geographic location. In Pakistan many shrines are decorated with blue tiles, and inside there may be decorative work with *shisha* (mirrors). The grave is covered with a green cloth and many flowers and garlands.

Moghul tombs in India are often white and peaceful. The Taj Mahal is an international symbol, although most people see it as a symbol of love rather than a building of spiritual significance.

Tombs and gardens fit an image of promised paradise. Used as a pleasure ground in life and an entrance to paradise at death, the garden is a living connection between heavenly and earthly realms. The trees planted are symbols: fruit trees symbolize life and cypresses symbolize death. The Moghul inscription on the Red Fort in Delhi

reads: "If there is paradise on earth, this is it, this is it, this is it."

In Iran, some tombs have twelve sides rather than the usual eight, symbolizing the twelve Shi'ah Imams.

Tombs and shrines are anathema to the unbending *jihadis,* the

ABOVE: The Taj Mahal shows the progression from square to dome.

fundamentalists; sadly, they have often damaged and destroyed them. Allah is compassionate and merciful, and Sufis show the loving side of their faith, serving others to escape their own selfishness. Hospices, hospitals, schools, and similar institutions are associated with Sufi teachers. The path they teach is a progress toward god.

In 1989, building work began on

the mausoleum of Ayatollah Khomeini, on a 5,000-acre (20 sqare km) site. The site is a vast rectangular plaza and the dome is supported by eight massive columns. There are two layers of upper windows decorated with tulips, symbols of martyrdom. A gilded dome covers the sarcophagus. On the floor lie scraps of paper on which visitors have written entreaties. There are educational facilities in the complex. The tomb is similar to any other Islamic tomb, but this one has parking for 20,000 cars and a shopping mall.

VIRGIN MARY

People did not need literacy to "read" a painting of the Holy Mother.

She wears blue clothes; blue paint was precious being expensive in Medieval times. Early Byzantine art shows her in royal purple, reserved for emperors and empresses.

The Cathédrale Notre Dame de Chartres in France has a stained glass window, *Notre Dame de la belle verrière*, dating from 1137. The alchemists must have worked hard to achieve the quality of the blue glass used to show the virgin against a red background. It is an object of veneration.

It is impossible not to be struck by the number of works that are *not* of the madonna and child: the annunciation, the immaculate conception, her assumption into heaven; her coronation with symbolic crown and, in some cases, with a halo of stars (oddly reminiscent of the symbol of the European Union), were all popular. Kariye Camii in Istanbul

shows a sequence of eighteen pictures of mainly apocryphal events in the life of the virgin. Jesus Christ is shown as an adult too, not always as a baby.

All artists used a wealth of symbolism in the flowers they painted around the Virgin Mary.

ABOVE: Altarpiece: the assumption of the Virgin Mary to heaven, Santa Maria del Popolo, Rome.

Roses symbolize her love and the scent in her opened tomb when she ascended into heaven. A medieval rose symbol has four petals, a motif still popular in quilting and embroidery.

Lilies symbolize purity and virginity. The Assumption Lily conveniently blossoms in August — the fifteenth being the celebration of Mary's assumption into heaven in Roman Catholic and Eastern churches.

The yellow iris (or flag) symbolizes the immaculate conception, and Mary as the Queen of Heaven. Lilies and irises are symbols of the seven sorrows she suffered — sad incidents in her life such as the flight into Egypt, the way of the cross, suffering, the death and burial of Christ. These sorrows are also symbolized as seven swords piercing her heart. Some paintings show just one sword, symbolizing her immaculate heart.

The blue periwinkle is an emblem that matches her clothing. The pansy is the "Trinity flower."

Strawberries, which flower and fruit simultaneously, symbolize fruitfulness.

Mary is often shown beside a cedar tree, noted for longevity and never decaying. This mirrors Mary's sin-free state and immortality. The cedar's scent and oil are believed to repel that great symbol of evil, the snake.

The pomegranate appears in some classic paintings, with the child offering seeds to the Holy Mother. Pomegranates, with their tightly packed seeds, symbolize fruitfulness and unity.

The month of May is particularly associated with Mary.

In an old story, a tabby cat was present in the stable at Bethlehem and the Virgin traced her initial on the animal's head. To this day, all tabbies bear an "M" on their heads, symbolizing the occasion.

THE WHITE HOUSE

All early American homes were not romantic log cabins. From the outset, homes were copies of those the settlers had left behind, and European architectural style remained paramount.

In Washington, the proposed presidential palace designed by Pierre L'Enfant was based on the style of French kings and ideas in vogue in Europe, but the grand design was too much in the style of autocrats for a developing democracy to embrace.

It was rejected in favor of a smaller mansion designed by Irishman James Hoban, who based his plan upon Leinster House in Dublin. Leinster House was then the home of a duke. Ironically, it became the seat of the Irish Parliament.

Hoban's house owed much to the Palladian style. Palladio's buildings harked back to classical Rome and sought to create calm and harmony. A Palladian villa is a statement of social class. Palladian-style buildings in Calcutta were for the *raj* (British ruling class), not the populace. The architectural historian Giles Worsley observed that many features, such as the portico, serliana, and the centrally planned villa, are symbols of dominance and authority, and of sovereignty.

The central planning of the villa incorporated symbolic shapes — the circle and square — that created harmonic proportions.

The pillars are towering and strong, and the portico is a barrier to welcome the powerful in and keep unwelcome strangers out.

A serliana is a Venetian window with three parts. The central window is the largest and is often arched. It is symbolically associated with the Roman emperors, the papacy, and the Trinity. The White House has a Venetian window in the East Room.

Clearly, the symbolism of the building did not appeal to all. People found the President's house too large and imposing and not a reflection of the political idealism of the founding fathers. John Adams thought of handing the house over to the Supreme Court and living a more republican life in a small house. However, he complied with the Residence Act of 1790 and moved into the new Presidential residence on November 1, 1800. The original house was not in fact white; it was painted white following a fire caused by British troops in 1812.

The White House gardens are no less symbolic. Jefferson was a keen gardener: the landscape was to embody the values and aspirations of the emerging democracy. He wanted a house, not a palace, and a garden rather than a park.

The new democracy succeeded in freeing itself from the traditions of the past, where absolute rulers lived, guarded behind high walls and gates, and where the powerful lived in fear of the people. In Washington, as far as was possible, house and garden were intent on symbolizing presidents as "first among equals" and creating public buildings that were exactly that — public. The White House was symbolic of the new republic and its presidency. To modern Americans it symbolizes freedom and democracy.

The house has grown, but the central part of the building remains untouched. A symbol of presidential power and American government so powerful, it does not surprise us to hear that "the White House has issued a statement…"

GLOSSARY

alchemy An ancient practice of attempting to turn base metals into gold.

allegory Symbolism used to represent truths about human existence.

amulet An object intended to bring good luck or protection to its owner.

avarice Greed.

deity A god or immortal being.

duality The state or idea that things are made up of two parts that are opposites.

emoticons A facial expression made up of punctuation and letters.

grimoire A textbook of magic.

hoax A story deliberately fabricated to mislead people.

horoscope An astrological diagram that uses the positions of planets and signs of the zodiac to infer a person's character traits.

iconographic Representing something by pictures or diagrams.

megalith A large stone used by prehistoric cultures as a monument or building rock.

menhir A single, upright monolith.

mosque A building used for worship by Muslims.

palmistry The practice of reading a person's character or future from the lines in his or her palms.

pyre A heap of materials used for burning a dead body, usually as part of a funeral rite.

runes Characters that are part of an ancient Germanic alphabet.

satire A literary work intended to poke fun at another work.

sundial An instrument that shows the time of day using shadows that indicate the location of the sun.

symbolism The use of objects as symbols representing a larger idea.

FOR MORE INFORMATION

American Federation of Astrologers
6535 S. Rural Road
Tempe, AZ 85283
(480) 838-1751
Web site: http://www.astrologers.com
Organization uniting astrologers who promote the art of astrology through research, teaching, and practice.

British Museum
Great Russell Street
London WC1B 3DG
England
Web site:
http://www.britishmuseum.org
A museum with a large array of art and artifacts from throughout human history.

Metropolitan Museum of Art
1000 Fifth Avenue
New York, NY 10028
(212) 535-7710
Web site: http://www.metmuseum.org
One of the world's largest and finest art museums with collections that include more than two million works of art spanning five thousand years of world culture, from prehistory to the present and from every part of the globe.

Victoria and Albert Museum
Cromwell Road
London SW7 2RL
England
Web site: http://www.vam.ac.uk
The world's greatest museum of art and design.

Visit Wiltshire
3 Rollestone Street
Salisbury, Wiltshire SP1 1DX
England
Web site:
http://www.visitwiltshire.co.uk/salisbury/home
Center of tourism for Salisbury, location of Stonehenge.

FOR MORE INFORMATION/FOR FURTHER READING

Yucatan Today **Magazine**
Calle 39 //183 x 54 and 56
Col. Centro, C.P. 97000
Merida, Yucatan
Mexico
(999) 927-8531
Web site: http://yucatantoday.com
A tourist's guide to visiting the
   Yucatan, which includes the
ruins of Chichen Itza, Izamal,
Mayapan, and others.

Web Sites

Due to the changing nature of Internet
links, Rosen Publishing has
developed an online list of Web sites
related to the subject of this book.
This site is updated regularly. Please
use this link to access the list:

http://www.rosenlinks.com/snat/super

FOR FURTHER READING

Battistini, Matilde. *Symbols and Allegories in Art*. Los Angeles, CA: J. Paul Getty Museum, 2005.

Blavatsky, H.P. *The Secret Doctrine*. New York, NY: Tarcher, 2009.

Brandes, Stanley. *Skulls to the Living, Bread to the Dead: The Day of the Dead in Mexico and Beyond*. Hoboken, NJ: Wiley-Blackwell, 2007.

Bruce-Mitford, Miranda. *The Illustrated Book of Signs and Symbols*. New York, NY: DK, 2008.

Buchholz, Elke Linda, Susanne Kaeppele, Karoline Hille, Irina Stotland, and Gerhard Buhler. *Art: A World History*. New York, NY: Abrams, 2007.

Cornwell, Hillarie and James Cornwell. *Saints, Signs, and Symbols: The Symbolic Language of Christian Art*. Harrisburg, PA: Morehouse, 2009.

Crenshaw, Paul. *Discovering the Great Masters: The Art Lover's Guide to Understanding Symbols in Paintings*. New York, NY: Universe, 2009.

Graham-Dixon, Andrew. *Art: Over 2,500 Works from Cave to Contemporary*. New York, NY: DK, 2008.

Hall, James. *Dictionary of Subject and Symbols in Art*. Boulder, CO: Westview Press, 2007.

Joseph, Frank. *Advanced Civilizations of Prehistoric America: The Lost Kingdoms of the Adena, Hopewell, Mississippians, and Anasazi*. Rochester, VT: Bear & Company, 2009.

Kaczynski, Richard. *Perdurabo: The Life of Aleister Crowley*. Berkeley, CA: North Atlantic Books, 2010.

Lehner, Ernst, and Johanna Lehner. *Astrology and Astronomy: A Pictorial Archive of Signs and Symbols*. Mineola, NY: Dover Publications, 2005.

Milner, George R. *The Moundbuilders: Ancient Peoples of Eastern North America*. West Sussex, UK: Thames & Hudson, 2005.

Strickland, Carol. *The Annotated Mona Lisa: A Crash Course in Art History from Prehistoric to Post-Modern*. Kansas City, MO: Andrews-McMeel, 2007.

Townsend, Richard F. *The Aztecs*. 3rd ed. West Sussex, UK: Thames & Hudson, 2009.

Wilder, Jesse Bryant. *Art History for Dummies*. Hoboken, NJ: Wiley, 2007.

Wilkins, David G. *The Collins Big Book of Art: From Cave Art to Pop Art*. New York, NY: Harper, 2005.

About the Author

Beryl Dhanjal was educated at the School of Oriental and African Studies in London and has worked as a librarian, a community worker, and a teacher at several British universities and colleges. She has written many books for children and teens. She lives with her husband in Tunbridge Wells, a town located on the Kent-Sussex border in England.